Yvonne Adams.

# COAST & COUNTRY COOKING

## 270 FAVOURITE RECIPES

COMPILED, EDITED AND ILLUSTRATED BY GAY CORRAN
CO-ILLUSTRATED BY YVONNE ADAMS

Published by Chalmers Holdings Ltd. In the year 2001 A D



Designed and edited by Gay Corran

Printed in England by Optichrome Ltd, Maybury Road, Woking, Surrey, GU21 5HX

ISBN Number: 0-9540445-0-9

Acknowledgement:

The frontispiece illustration of Lulworth Castle by Yvonne Adams is used with the kind permission of Mr and Mrs Wilfrid Weld.

# Dedication

This book is dedicated to all the lesser saints, fishers of men, who are doing great things around the Benefice, and, naturally, to Saints Andrew, Christopher, Nicholas, and to the Holy Trinity.

## About This Book

One of the first sermons given by our new priest-in-charge, Bob Naylor, after his licensing service was on the subject of hospitality. The sharing of food and drink was, he said, important for the spiritual side of human beings, as well as essential to life. It is an appropriate thought for us, living as we do in this very beautiful part of Dorset, for we attract many families, friends and holiday makers to visit us at home and in our excellent hotels, restaurants and pubs. However, the idea of a Coast and Country Cookbook was born because we were looking for a way to help support and keep open the four churches of our Benefice. By buying this book and its associated recipe cards, and, better still, by giving it to all your friends and family, you are helping to keep our churches alive and financially healthy. Thus they will remain, not only historically significant, as the lovely old buildings they certainly are, but also at the real heart of the lives of all of us who use or visit them, whether seldom or often.

The recipes are attributed to the people who offered them: they may be original or gleaned from various sources, and perhaps modified, by the donors. They might be old family favourites or newly discovered on travels abroad. I have edited them only so that they conform to modern systems of weights and measures and to a consistent format.

There are many vegetarian recipes, which, on the advice of our publisher, who eats fish but not meat, I have scattered throughout the book, rather than concentrated into one section. There are also many recipes, suitable for gluten-free diets, which use no wheat, oats or rye flour. All the Tidal Favourites can be made with Valpiform gluten-free pastry mix flour substituted for normal flour, where called for. Good Chemists shops can obtain this for you: it is expensive, but worth it if, like me, you cannot eat gluten.

I am extremely grateful to Yvonne Adams for allowing me to use her beautiful watercolour paintings, listed on page four. The rest are my own, except for a few images that I borrowed from various sources in the public domain. I must also own to all the Tidal Favourites recipes, My Mother Said… and, I'm afraid, to any and all mistakes.

I thank Giles Marsh and all the churchwardens, who gathered in the recipes, and Sue Bartholomew who gave us our title as well; also Trish Rudd for her help with the proof reading. I especially thank all the contributors for their wonderful recipes, and for the time and trouble they took over them. I regret that it has not been possible personally to make and test every one of them – yet!

Publication of this book, in the form it finally took, would not have been possible without Sam Chalmers' interest, enthusiasm and involvement.

Happy eating, and, as we say in Dorset, come again soon!

Gay Corran

*Tides, West Lulworth, Dorset, BH20 5RS* GayCorran@tides.freeserve.co.uk

***The book "Coast and Country Cooking" and associated recipe cards are sold in aid of church funds for the Benefice of East and West Lulworth, Chaldon Herring and Winfrith Newburgh, Purbeck, Dorset, England.***

## Publisher's Foreword

I first met the Corrans five years ago: Andrew in the drive, and Gay soon afterwards in the kitchen of Tides. As their newly arrived neighbour, this was to be the first of many meetings. Sometimes it was as a weary traveller reaching the cliff top at Lulworth after a long journey; sometimes to escape from the lack of convenience of a house in the throes of a major restoration programme; sometimes just to enjoy the company of two busy people who believe, as I do, that the evolution of the human hand was entirely predicated on the shape of a wine glass; sometimes, if I was caught unawares, to be frisked for an idle cheque book to support yet another fund-raising scheme; but always to be rewarded with, surely, the best view from any house in England, day or night, and food and hospitality commensurate with it.

This book is a product of Gay in full flight, computer mouse in one hand, paint brush in the other, spatula between her teeth, and about her the determined mien of a professional fund-raiser; a sort of cross between a fairy god-mother and a Chieftain tank.

As a schoolboy in a small Wiltshire village in the nineteen fifties, I was a compulsive scribbler. The wife of the local squire, who had a reputation as a clairvoyant, told my mother that one day I would publish a successful book. I hadn't expected that this might be a book of recipes; however, if it sells in enormous numbers, and raises large amounts of money, I will be proud to have been associated with it.

Coast and Country Cooking is full of fun and good eating. Buy one for yourself and half a dozen for your friends! Then we shall all profit from the prophecy and benefit the Benefice.

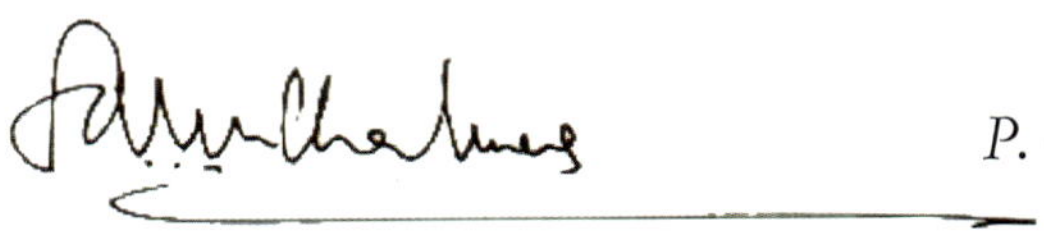

*P. O. Box 12070, Dubai, United Arab Emirates*

**Looking West**

# Contents

# Illustrations by Yvonne Adams

# Brunch and Lunch

**Lulworth Cove**

## Quotations

There is no snooze button on a cat who wants breakfast. *Anon*

The critical period in matrimony is breakfast time. *A P Herbert*

Once a woman has forgiven a man she must not re-heat his sins for breakfast.
*Marlene Dietrich*

My wife and I tried to breakfast together. We had to stop or our marriage would have been wrecked. *Winston Churchill*

Why, sometimes, I've believed as many as six impossible things before breakfast!
*Alice in Wonderland, Lewis Carroll*

## Broad Beans Spanish Style – Tidal Favourites

We first came across this classic Spanish dish in a beautiful old mill restaurant somewhere in the hills behind Ronda, in Southern Spain. There are many variations, and they are all good. Fresh little beans straight out of the garden are best of all, but packets of baby frozen ones also work well. The tang provided by the bacon can be obtained by using Serrano ham, or any ham-type chunks that you can get hold of. Quantities are variable, too: can you imagine a Spanish Mama sticking rigidly to exact measurements in a book? However, give it a go with roughly these allowances for four people:

1 *packet baby frozen broad beans*
*1 or two packets of frozen lardons, or streaky smoked bacon, or bits of ham, chopped small*
*½ an onion, or more*
*1 or 2 cloves of garlic, chopped*
*Grated zest of 1 lemon*
*Cream or crème fraîche, to finish*
*Sea salt and black pepper*
*Olive oil*
*Chopped parsley or chives, to garnish*

Boil the frozen or fresh beans in salted water for a minute or two, until tender: drain and set aside. Soften the onion and then the garlic in a frying pan in a little olive oil. Add the bacon or ham and fry until crisp. (If you don't like your onions caramelised, remove them and set aside before cooking the bacon.) Combine all the other ingredients in the pan, using enough cream to bring the dish to the consistency you like, season well, and serve with a sprinkle of chopped parsley over each helping. It might be unconventional, but if you were feeding a hungry mob, you could always perch a poached or fried egg on top, for a more substantial brunch…

## American Pie Topping – Sally Lee

This will cover any casserole dish.

*75g (1/4 lb) margarine, melted in 275ml (8 fl oz) (1 cup) milk*
*150g (5oz) (1 cup) self-raising flour*
*1/2 teaspoon baking powder*

Measure roughly – mix roughly – leave it all lumpy and messy. Add any herbs if you wish. Cover your casserole with it and bake at 160C (350F) for thirty to forty minutes.

A good quickie is to mix cooked chicken pieces with your favourite condensed soup (undiluted), cover with messy pie topping and bake…. Delicious!

## Bacon Floddie – Kevin Booker

Ideal for a starter, light lunch or supper dish, I have slightly updated this Olde Englishe omelette. I would serve it with a crisp salad and a Red Onion Marmalade.

*2-3 eggs*
*1 rasher smoked bacon*
*1 medium sized mushroom*
*1 medium potato*
*50g (2oz) butter*
*125ml (4oz) vegetable oil*
*Black pepper*

Cut the bacon into strips and fry in a little oil until crisp. Slice and add the mushroom to the bacon and cook for a minute more. Cut the potato into matchsticks and fry until crisp: drain and dry on kitchen paper.

In a mixing bowl crack the eggs and add the bacon, mushroom and potato sticks. Combine with a fork and season with pepper only, as the bacon will add sufficient salt to this dish. Heat a non-stick frying pan and add a few knobs of butter. When the butter is frothy add the egg mixture. Allow to set, stirring two or three times and cleaning down the sides of the pan.

Now comes the clever bit! Remove all pets and children from the kitchen and flip the omelette over. (Good luck!)

Cook for about two minutes and remove the pan from the heat. Allow the omelette to stand for about a minute before serving.

## Basic Gluten-free Pastry – Tidal Favourites
## (Also works for normal pastry)

One of the greatest treats you can give a Coeliac is a gluten-free pie or quiche, as they are completely out of bounds made with normal pastry. Valpiform pastry flour makes absolutely delicious tender pastry, upon which you will receive compliments from everyone, Coeliac or not. The Chemist at Wool can get it for you, given a couple of days' notice. (Be warned: it is expensive, although not compared with the price of eating out, or even with buying a round of drinks, not that I'm knocking either…) The recipe works equally well with plain flour, or half and half-wholemeal and plain. This quantity will line and cover a 20cm (8") pie dish, or line a 30cm (12") flan dish, with some extra for little ones.

Put in a large bowl:

*455g (1 lb) Valpiform Pastry Flour, or plain white flour, or half wholemeal/half white flours*
*225g (8oz) Trex*
*Teaspoon salt*

Cut the Trex into the flour with two knives, until the mix looks like petits pois. Work quickly, and keep plenty of air in it by scooping it up from the bottom of the bowl with your knives. Add just enough *cold water*, stirred in with a knife, to make the dough hold together. Still working quickly and lightly, scoop the dough into a ball, pat Valpiform (or plain) flour all over it, and put the ball into the middle of a Valpi-floured (plain) board. At this stage, halve the mix if you are making a normal-sized covered pie. Using a Valpi-floured (plain) rolling pin and a light hand, roll the dough out to roughly the size and shape of your pie dish. Gently put the rolling pin on the pastry and roll the dough over it; quickly seize your dish and unroll the pastry into it. It is very tender at this stage; don't be alarmed if it doesn't look fit for a cookery book photograph. Just patch it up, safe in the knowledge that you'll get Brownie points for your light and crunchy pastry. Fill with whatever you like, and roll out the second half in the same way. Unroll it over your filling, neaten the edges, brush with milk for a gloss, and bake until golden, at180C (350F). This will probably take about 45 minutes.

Suggestions for fillings:

*Blackberries (we grow wonderful ones in Dorset) with sugar to taste.*
*3 or 4 cooking apples, peeled, cored and sliced; about 250g (8oz) sugar; sprinkle of allspice.*
*Washed sliced rhubarb; sugar; candied ginger, chopped small, with some of its syrup.*

## Brunch Baked Potato – Linda Brewer

Serves four.

*4 jacket potatoes (either baked in the oven or microwaved)*
*225g (8oz) smoked bacon*
*2 leeks*
*125g tub of soured cream*

Cut the bacon into small pieces and stir fry with the sliced leeks until cooked. Cut each potato in half and fluff up the surface using a fork. Spoon the bacon and leek mixture onto the top. Place a dessertspoonful of soured cream on top of each potato and serve.

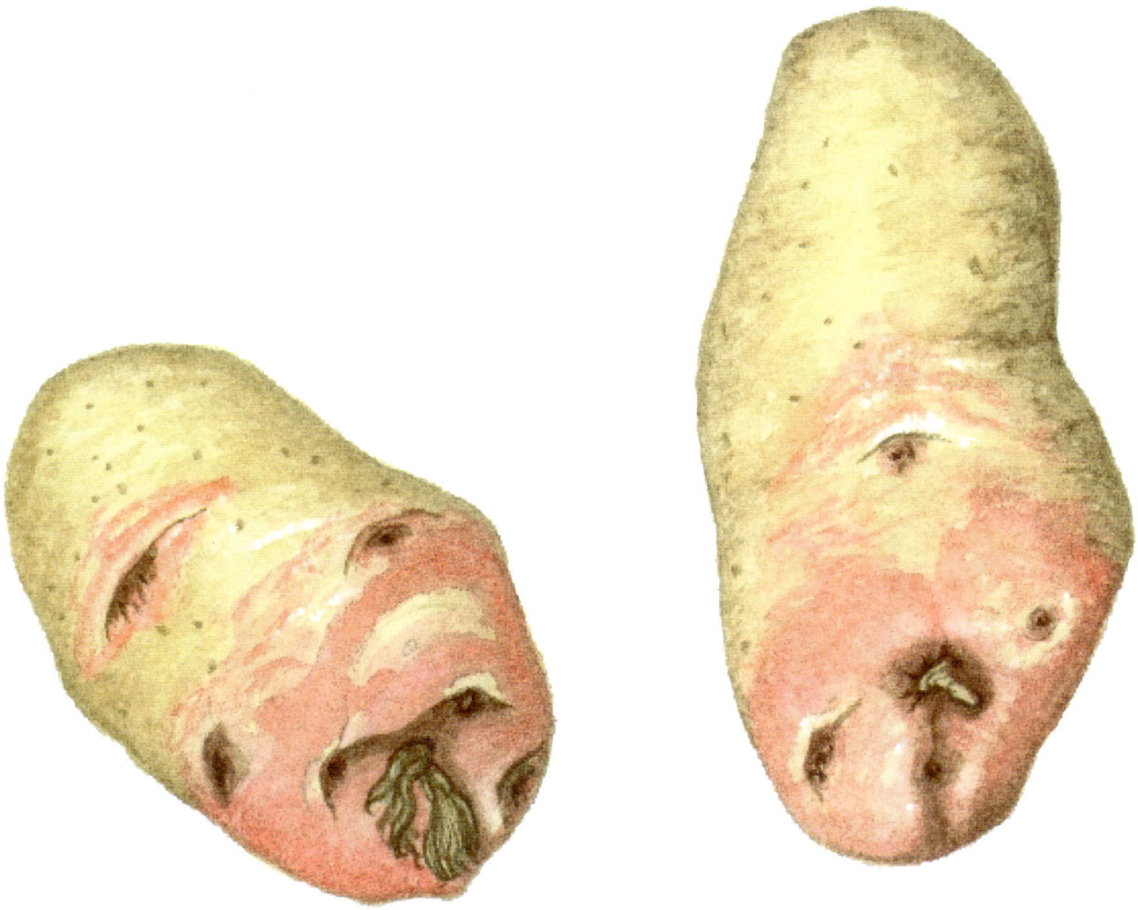

## Sally Lee's Tips

**Tomatoes:** Stroke a ripe tomato with the blade of a knife to peel easily.

## Cassoulet – Geoffrey Donald

This recipe hails from the region of France just to the north of the Pyrenees, the Haute Garonne and Languedoc, a land of mediaeval cathedrals, Cathar castles, ancient heresies and burnings at the stake. Like many provincial French dishes it has local variations and relies very much on what is at hand, traditionally mutton, goose and fatty pork, but also 'confit'... poultry preserved with herbs in its own fat... and herb sausages. The vehicle for the meats is a generous quantity of haricot beans... essential for filling up the working man! After the ingredients have been prepared they are built up in layers in a tall earthenware casserole (without lid) and cooked slowly in the oven. Traditionally, a topping of breadcrumbs absorbs the fat as it rises through the liquids and then browns to a crust. It does take a little time to put together... perhaps old Granny could spend a leisurely afternoon in the farmhouse kitchen... but if you make plenty it freezes well for future use.

There are three stages to the preparation: the beans, the meats and the final layering in the casserole, so there are two opportunities for a break until later. Do not stint on the beans or the herbal flavourings. The choice of meats is up to the individual, but there should be some variety and traditionally lamb and poultry is included. Don't use red meats such as stewing steaks and the denser cuts of pork, as they tend to be a little heavy and do not absorb the herbal flavours well. Traditionally, large quantities of goose and pork fat and rind were included! Perhaps this would be drastically reduced these days... again it is up to the cook to decide how fatty the meats are to be.

Serves about eight to ten. Quantities can be varied at will.

*900g (2 lb) dried white kidney beans*
*500ml (1 pint) or more chicken stock*
*2 or 3 medium onions, peeled and cut in quarters*
*2 or 3 sticks celery, cut into inch lengths*
*3 or 4 carrots, medium sliced*
*3 cloves garlic, cut into two or three pieces*
*Bouquet garni or mixed herbs*
*Sprig of fresh rosemary (or thyme)*
*2 large onions, peeled and sliced small*
*Tin of peeled tomatoes or a good squirt of purée*
*3 or 4 herb sausages (or even smoked ones)*
*225g (half pound) lean bacon (more if liked)*
*Cup dry white wine*
*Salt and black pepper*
*Olive oil to help in the sauté*
*Breadcrumbs*

Cassoulet, continued

As mentioned above, the meats and quantities are open to choice. Suggestions, all off the bone:

*900g (2 lb) lean lamb*
*450g (1 lb) pork, lean or fatty, with or without rind*
*450g (1 lb) chicken or duck breasts*

**Part one**:

Soak the beans overnight in plenty of unsalted water. Pour this away and rinse them. Cover in fresh water and bring to a simmer. Spoon off any foam that floats to the surface and continue to do this until no more forms. Discard the water and rinse again thoroughly. Put the beans into a large pan and add enough of the stock to cover well. Pierce the sausages several times with a fork and add these, together with the pork. Bring to a simmer for a few minutes and spoon off any scum and fat that rises to the surface. Now add the onion quarters, garlic pieces, bouquet garni or mixed herbs, rosemary sprig, salt and pepper. **Do not stir!** Natural convection during the simmering will dissipate the flavours. Simmer gently for about 30 minutes and then carefully remove and reserve the sausage before it starts to go mushy inside. Continue simmering for a further 40 minutes or so to tenderise the beans; remove from the heat and fish out the onions, garlic, bouquet garni, rosemary sprig, excess fat and any other undesirable bits and pieces. Now add the other meats, cut only into two or three large pieces and simmer for a further 30 minutes, adding more stock if necessary. By now the beans will be well cooked and the meats will have picked up the herb flavours. At this point the pan can be left overnight if desired, when the flavours will develop further.

**Part two**:

Remove the meats from the beans. Pour off and reserve the liquids and keep the beans in the pan for later. Cut the bacon into inch size squares and sauté in a frying pan until crisp; reserve. If you like pork rind, this can be cut from the meat and similarly browned, but take great care as you put damp meat into the hot pan. Cut the other meats into inch cubes and fry these too in batches. Make sure you are really searing the meats in hot oil or fat and not just boiling them in their juices (note the difference between steam and a light smoke!). If so, pour off the excess liquid into the reserved stock and perhaps add more oil. Put all the browned meats to one side.

Now sauté the sliced onions in the same pan. They will pick up the brown glaze from the meat so the usual 'transparent' look will be difficult to distinguish. Pour in the wine and boil quite vigorously to drive off the alcohol and reduce the liquids. Scrape all into an ovenproof casserole, add the celery, carrots, the tin of tomatoes, and, if you like, the pieces of garlic discarded earlier, a couple of bay leaves and perhaps a touch more herbs. Add the diced meats, enough of the reserved stock to cover and cook gently in an oven at about 160C (320F) for an hour. At the end of this time, remove the garlic, bay leaves and any excess fat. This is a second suitable moment to postpone until later.

**Part three**:

The cassoulet is finally assembled in layers in a tall, narrow earthenware pot. If this is too wide the layers will not build up thickly enough. If necessary, carefully heat the ingredients through again; spoon a good layer of beans into the pot. Follow this with a layer of the meats, plus the sausage cut into half-inch slices. Continue with another layer of beans, then meats, until the pot is full or all is used up. Try to get a little of everything into each layer. Finally, pour in enough of the stock liquids to just reach the surface. At this point the traditional breadcrumb layer should be added to soak up the rising fats and then be exposed to the heat of the oven to brown to a crust. Cook in a hot oven, about 180C, (350F) for an hour and a quarter, adding more stock as needed to keep it just at the surface. Serve in a deep soup bowl with a green side-salad.

## Chicken and Broccoli Layer – Trish Rudd

Easy peasy and absolutely delicious: everyone will think you're a genius in the kitchen!

*75ml (3 fl oz) milk*
*10g (½ oz) butter*
*10g (½ oz) breadcrumbs*
*150ml (¼ pint) tin condensed cream of celery soup*
*½ level teaspoon curry powder*
*½ teaspoon lemon juice*
*110g (4oz) broccoli*
*Salt and pepper*
*225g (6-8oz) boned, skinned chicken breast*

Melt butter in a small saucepan, stir in breadcrumbs and cook for about one minute.

Layer the chicken in an ovenproof dish with the broccoli. Mix soup, curry powder and lemon juice together; fill half the soup tin with milk and add to the mix. Pour over the chicken and broccoli. Sprinkle the breadcrumbs over the top and bake in the oven at 200C (400F) for half an hour and at 180C (250F) for a further half hour.

You can add grated cheese to the breadcrumbs when you sprinkle, which I think makes it even yummier.

## Chicken and Leek Pie – Trish Rudd

Pastry:

*175g (6oz) (Valpiform pastry mix for Gluten free) or half wholemeal/half plain flour for "normals"*
*40g (1 ½ oz) butter*
*40g (1 ½ oz) lard*

Blend together until breadcrumb like, but a little moister. Add some water, a very little at a time, until the mixture holds together but do not make it sticky and too doughy.

Filling:

*Crushed or chopped ginger, as much as you like*
*1 fillet of chicken, sliced*
*1 small shallot*
*1 small clove of garlic, chopped*
*Olive oil and butter as needed*
*1 floret of broccoli*
*1 medium sized carrot*
*1 large leek, sliced*

Put the vegetables into boiling, salted water (Just enough to cover them), for no more than 5 minutes. Do not throw away the water. Heat a little oil and butter, add the ginger, shallot and garlic and sauté for a few seconds. Add the chicken and stir fry until brown. Then add the vegetables and their water; mix all this together adding salt and pepper, to taste. Cook for a further few minutes and then thicken with a little cornflour.
Roll out two-thirds of the pastry and place in the bottom of a well-greased pie dish. Pour chicken mixture into the dish. Roll out the remaining pastry and cover the mixture. Brush a little milk over the top of the pastry and stab a hole into the top.
Place in an oven Mark 4 (350F/180C) until the pastry is golden brown on top.

## Corned Beef Hash – Geoffrey Donald

This is a favourite American way of turning leftover potatoes into a meal in itself. It will also freeze effectively for those quick warm-up occasions.

> *In almost any proportions, but around 50:50 is about right: Tin or tins of Fray Bentos, or similar, corned beef. Mashed potatoes.*

If the potatoes are not already mashed they may need cooking in boiling water just a little longer to loosen the texture before mashing. The usual dash of milk and salt can be added if desired. Empty in the corned beef, dice up and mix in. The mixture now needs to be carefully heated through thoroughly, but since there is practically no liquid present it is vital to keep the mixture on the move and the heat not too high. The corned beef will exude some melted fat and juices and this will ease the mixing. When nicely hot it is ready to serve. For a warm-up it can be microwaved, carefully pan - heated or added to the frying pan. If you like a crust, *rösti* style, fry the mixture in plenty of olive oil and butter, in a non-stick pan, until crisp and golden underneath.

## Great Scrambled Eggs – Sam Chalmers

This is a brunch idea I picked up a few years ago at The Vinegar Factory in New York, a brunch room-cum-gourmet marketplace on the Eastside. The recipe is as I wrote it down at the time.

*110g (4oz) butter*
*24 large organic eggs*
*225g (8oz) cream cheese,*
*Chives, finely chopped*

Melt 4oz butter in a dutch-oven type casserole. (A heavy-bottomed Le Creuset style casserole is suitable.) Beat 2 dozen large organic eggs in a round bowl. Add 8oz cream cheese, cut into small pieces, to the eggs. Pour the egg mixture into the melted butter and cook over a very low heat, stirring constantly until the eggs begin to set. Turn off the heat, since the eggs will continue to cook. Garnish with finely chopped chives and serve directly from the pot. Accompany with:

*Orange juice, coffee and tea.*
*Baskets of sliced breads, bagels, muffins, Danish pastries and croissants.*
*Cheeses, butter, jams (I prefer marmalade) and honey.*
*Platters of smoked fish, sliced tomatoes, cucumbers and red onions.*

## Grandmother's Remedies – Sally Lee

Eat slowly – live long.

## **Liverpool Scouse,** as prepared by the Priest-in-Charge – **Bob Naylor**

Every so often, to the horror and dread of the residents and staff of the Stable Family Home Trust, I used to declare a day to be "The Stables Scouse Day".

My secretary, who is also a Scouser, and I taught people how to talk proper and we all had a lorra, lorra fun, part of which involved me acting as cook and preparing this dish for fifty people.

The first time I did this, and cooked the Scouse, I asked one of the residents assisting me in the preparation of this gastronomic delight, to remove her sock, for the addition of such an article of clothing always adds a touch of "je ne sais quoi" to any dish.

With a deft sleight of hand, common to all Scousers, the sock disappeared down the sleeve of my cook's apron, but deceived the resident completely, she being convinced that the sock had been added to the Scouse.

At 12.30pm, lunch was served. At 12.45pm, fifty people began to eat, only after a thorough search of their plates lasting a full quarter of an hour, and still not entirely convinced that carrot was indeed carrot, and not the remains of material which could have come from a sock.

At 2.00pm I returned Emma's sock to her!

For those of you who like to flavour your Scouse with a sock, I can recommend it, having used one many times, giving a distinct flavour to the dish – especially when accompanied by a rather naughty glass of red wine. Other tried and tested flavourings include the inner sole of an old shoe (recommended by Cilla Black), the feathers from a tickling stick (much favoured by Ken Dodd), and six Everton mints (remove the wrapping first, of course). The latter has been very popular with Everton FC over the years, and Walter Smith, the club's present manager, has been very happy to continue the tradition, feeling that a plate of Scouse flavoured in this way is as good as a goal start in any game.

Do try it, with or without the additional flavouring. It's the gear!

Feeds four generously, and the result will be a full stomach and an instant Scouse accent as appealing as mine.

*1 large tin of Corned Dog (Corned Beef if no dog willing or available)*
*2 large onions*
*6 carrots (any other vegetables may be tossed into the pot)*
*Approximately 1.35 kg (3 lb) potatoes*
*Water*
*2 Oxo cubes*

Put the corned dog and vegetables into a stockpot or large saucepan. Fill up to the brim with the peeled and sliced potatoes. Fill to one inch from the top with cold water. Sprinkle two Oxo cubes over the top. Bring to the boil and simmer for one hour.
Note: all cooking to be done on top of the cooker and not in the oven.

## Marmalade – Margaret Whitehouse

Makes approximately 3.2 kg, or 7 lbs, in the terms of the era when I learnt to make it.

*700g (1½ lbs) Seville oranges*
*1 large sweet orange*
*½ large lemon*
*2.50 litres (4½ pints) water*
*2kg (4½ lbs) sugar*

**Step one:** Scrub the oranges and lemon, dry well and cut in half. Squeeze out the juice and strain into a large bowl. Place pips on a small muslin square and tie with string to form bag. Use a sharp stainless steel knife to cut skin, rind and pith in thin slices. (Or put in liquidiser cut in pieces.)

**Step two:** Put shredded peel into bowl with juice and bag of pips. Add the cold water. Cover with a clean cloth and stand over night. Next day, turn contents of bowl into preserving pan and simmer very gently for about two hours or until peel is quite tender and the liquid has been much reduced.

**Step three:** Remove bag of pips, squeeze out liquid. Stir in preserving crystals or granulated sugar and allow to dissolve over gentle heat. When dissolved, and not before, bring to full rolling boil. Continue to boil hard for about twenty to twenty five minutes until setting point is reached.

**Step four:** To test for set: Put a spoonful of the marmalade on a saucer and leave in a cold place for one minute to cool, (or pop into fridge). The marmalade should crinkle when pushed with a finger. (Bet you lick it!) Turn down the heat while testing for set; otherwise it may overcook and pass the setting point.

**Step five:** remove pan from the heat and allow ten minutes to cool. Have ready clean, dry, warmed jars. Stir the marmalade well to distribute peel. Use a small jug or cup to fill the jars. Cover at once with waxed circles. When cold cover tops and label clearly. Store in a cool dry cupboard. Keeps well if you don't let anyone see it…

## Oeufs en Cocotte – Tidal Favourites

If any at your table dislike garlic, this is still good without the Boursin cream cheese; but the flavour is mild, and adds to the wickedness of this non-slimming starter or lunch dish.

Put into buttered ramekins, per person, in the following order:

*1 (free range) egg*
*A dollop of Boursin garlic and fines herbes cheese*
*Single or double cream, (seasoned with sea salt, black pepper, Tabasco,) about 2/3 way up dish*
*Finely snipped parsley*
*Grated cheddar, to cover*

Put the filled ramekins into a baking pan, and pour enough cold water into it to come about 1/3 way up the little pots. Bake in the oven at 150C (300F) for ten to fifteen minutes, or until the whites are just set. You can test with a knife, or shake the pan. Too much wobble and the whites will still be jelly, too little and the yolks will be hard. Everyone always wants more, but one is enough for a starter. Hearty appetites would get through two at lunch, though, served with a salad.

## Rosemary Flatbread – Sarah Pearce

My daughter Daisy likes this bread so much that I have to make two at a time.

*1 kg (2 lb) strong white flour*
*Pinch of salt*
*2 sachets dried yeast*
*500ml (18 fl oz) warm water*
*1 teaspoon sugar*
*150ml (1/4 pint) olive oil*
*Sea salt*
*Fresh rosemary*

Put the flour and a pinch of salt into a bowl. Make a well in the centre. Even when using dried yeast, I mix it with some of the warm water and a teaspoon of sugar and leave it to froth up. Pour the yeast mixture into the flour and stir with a wooden spoon. Add four tablespoons of olive oil and the rest of the warm water. Then knead the dough with your hands for ten to fifteen minutes – until you have a smooth and elastic dough. Roll it in a little olive oil and place in a bowl covered with a damp cloth in a warm spot. Leave for at least an hour, until the dough has doubled in size.

Punch it down and knead again. Divide it into two balls and roll each out on a floured surface to a thickness of one centimetre. Put them onto two oiled baking sheets. Brush all over with olive oil and sprinkle with sea salt and sprigs of fresh rosemary. Make dents with the handle of a wooden spoon all over the loaves.

Let the dough rise again for half-an-hour, having placed the baking sheets inside large oiled carrier bags. Bake in the oven for about twenty minutes at 200C (400F, gas mark 6) until golden brown. Brush with olive oil and eat warm.

## Perfect Pizza – Linda Brewer

Serves four.

*Pizza Base Mix*
*Tomato purée*
*110g (4oz) smoked wafer thin ham*
*110g (4oz) mushrooms*
*1 green pepper*
*1 small onion*
*175 g (6oz) grated cheese*
*1 large tomato*
*1 teaspoon oregano or mixed herbs*

Make up pizza base as manufacturer instructs. Cover base of pizza with tomato purée. Layer smoked ham so that the purée is covered. Arrange in layers the sliced mushrooms, diced pepper and chopped onion. Cover with the grated cheese and place the sliced tomato to decorate. Sprinkle over the oregano or mixed herbs and bake in a hot oven, 190C (375F) for about forty minutes. Serve with a mixed salad.

## Quick Pizza Base – Sally Lee

*225g (8oz) plain flour*
*Pinch salt*

Mix with:

*75ml (3 fl oz) oil*
*75ml (3 fl oz) boiling water*

Put into fridge for thirty minutes. Roll out, using lots of flour. Covers one large or two small plates.

Topping:

*Tomato purée or chopped pieces*
*Grated cheese, mushrooms, pineapple, bacon bits or what you will*

Bake at 160C (350F) for half an hour.

## Quiche For Real Men – Tidal Favourites

Although this recipe is gluten free if made with Valpiform Pastry Mix, it works equally well with your preferred flour if you are not cooking for a Coeliac. Quiche is forbidden food for Coeliacs at pubs and parties, so a home made gluten-free one straight out of the oven, hot, golden, cheesy, with a crisp crust, is a great gift. My family ask for it often, for weekend lunches and picnics, especially my husband, who adores it. Men don't come realer than my spouse, so we'll have no nonsense on that score!

Use the **Basic Pastry** mix and method, but add *165g (6oz) or so of strong cheddar, grated,* to the flour and Trex before cutting in. Roll the pastry into a good large pie dish, (about 30 cm or 12") building up the sides so as not to let the filling overflow. Any offcuts of pastry will make good individual quichelets, ideal for starters, especially if you put a few shrimps in the bottom of them before topping them up with the eggy mixture. Put the pastry case to bake at 180C (350F) while you make the filling, which is likely to take about 20 minutes.

In a pan (I find a wok-type is quickest), fry, chopped quite small:

*1 onion*
*2 cloves garlic*
*1 small red or orange pepper*
*275g (10oz) bacon, preferably smoked streaky (leave this out for vegetarians)*
*(Mushrooms are good, if liked, or shellfish for a fishy quiche or quichelets, but neither is essential).*

While these soften, stir occasionally to prevent burning, and prepare the cheesy custard. Into a bowl, put:

*4 large eggs (free-range if possible)*
*1 packet Boursin garlic and fines herbes soft cheese*
*570ml (1 pint) whole milk*
*Palmful sea salt*
*Dash each of Tabasco and Worcester sauce, or more, to taste*
*Several grinds black pepper*

Whisk well. Take the pastry case out of the oven when it is just turning pale gold, and cover the bottom with the onion/bacon mix. Grate over this:

*225gr (8oz) seriously strong cheddar cheese* (very butch)

Snip some fresh herbs, such as *Oregano or Parsley* over the cheese, and then pour the eggy mixture over the lot. Into the oven with it, until all is golden brown and you can't resist it any longer. (About 45 minutes at 180C, 350F) Ingredients and quantities for the filling can be varied according to what everyone likes and what you have available, but don't stint on the cheese. Serve it with a green salad dressed in an olive oil vinaigrette, or pack it into a basket to take on a picnic somewhere with a view and a bottle of wine, and the world will look good.

### Grandmother's Remedies – Sally Lee

**Gnat Bites:** Rub with a piece of soap to soothe.

## Stuffed Marrow – Brian (Gaffer) Rodgers

This is my favourite recipe. I have always wanted to cook marrows that grew in my garden for this recipe. For years our marrows failed but last year we had our best year ever, and I can recall eating nineteen of them and that excludes the ones we gave away. This explains why there are many variations of filling; in fact, you can put more than one type of filling in a single marrow to suit individual tastes.

Choose any of the following and season to taste:

*Mashed potato*
*Corned beef*
*Minced beef*
*Minced chicken*
*Cooked vegetables*

Peel the marrow and cut off the top throughout its length to form a lid. Scoop out the seeds and fill it with your chosen mixture. Replace the lid and put it in a roasting tin. Brush with butter or seasoned oil. Cook for one-and-a-half-hours at 200C (400F, gas mark 6). Cut into portions and serve with brown gravy sauce or chicken sauce.

## Tuna Fish Pie – Tidal Favourites

Tinned tuna is a wonderful standby, and this mixture also uses that other store-cupboard favourite, chopped tinned tomatoes. Fresh tomatoes, especially if you have a glut in the garden, are even nicer, though. As a pie, it makes an excellent lunch dish, served with a green salad, but the filling is also good simply poured over brown rice or pasta.

Make pastry as for Basic Pastry, adding grated cheese, as for Quiche. Roll out half, and bake blind until just turning gold. While it bakes, make the filling:

*1 large onion*
*4 cloves garlic*
*2 red, yellow or orange peppers*
*Olive oil, to fry vegetables*
*2 tins (dolphin-friendly) tuna fish*
*800g (2 standard tins) chopped tomatoes, or use fresh ones*
*80g (1 small packet) Boursin garlic and herb soft cheese*
*2 tablespoons (or a good large squirt) tomato puree*
*1 dessertspoon French mustard*
*1 dessertspoon honey*
*1 dessertspoon brown sugar*
*Tabasco or cayenne pepper – a dash, or more*
*A sprinkle of coriander leaf, fresh or dried*
*Sea salt, Worcester sauce, black pepper, to season*

Chop onion and fry in olive oil. Chop garlic and peppers and add to pan. When softened, add all the other ingredients and stir while simmering. Taste for seasoning and pour into the semi-baked pie shell. Roll out the second half of the pastry, and cover the pie with it. Brush with milk for a gloss, and bake at 180C (350F) for half an hour or so.
You can experiment with quantities and seasonings, adding or subtracting almost anything to your taste; hot and spicy works well and plentiful fresh herbs are good too.
It is very good-tempered, and will stay in the oven for much longer at a lower temperature, and can be eaten hot, cold or in between.

**My Mother Said…**

Always wash your hands before starting work in the kitchen, and change the towels often.

## Warm Scallop and Chicken Salad – Trish Rudd

A really very simple but effective dish, this is ideal for a summer lunch for about eight people. Start with the salad:

*1 Iceberg lettuce, shredded, or about 8 Little Gem hearts, broken into leaves*
*2 tomatoes, halved and quartered*
*One handful of pumpkin or sunflower seeds*
*1 bunch of watercress*
*1 bunch of spring onions, cleaned and sliced*
*1 green, 1 yellow and 1 red pepper, sliced*
*Half a cucumber, diced*
*Vinaigrette, or lemon juice and black pepper*

Put all ingredients except vinaigrette into an extremely large salad bowl. Then do the chicken and scallop bit:

*Approximately 4-6 cleaned scallops per person*
*4 boned chicken breasts, diced to about the same size as scallops*
*1 tablespoon sun-dried tomatoes*
*2 or 3 cloves of garlic, crushed*
*Fresh oregano, parsley or tarragon, to taste*
*1 tablespoon olive oil and 1 tablespoon butter*

Gently heat the oil and fry the chicken, with garlic, until golden brown. Remove from pan. Add butter to pan; as soon as it melts toss in the scallops and cook for about 2 minutes, stirring all the time. Sprinkle on the oregano and cook for a few more minutes until the scallops are opaque; put with the chicken. Stir-fry the sun-dried tomatoes in the pan for a couple of minutes, and pour over chicken and scallops. Stir the whole lot together and add, still warm, to your salad, which you have just tossed with the vinaigrette. Serve immediately.

## Pizza – Susan Marsh

Many years ago Giles and I spent our summers hitch-hiking around Europe. It was the thing to do in those halcyon student days. Amazingly, in this day and age of fast food from countries all over the world, neither of us had eaten pizza until we arrived in Milan, Italy. We were both eighteen at the time! Authentic Italian food whetted our appetites; pizza is a firm family favourite, especially with our two daughters who are vegetarians. This is a recipe that the children used to love to make when they were little. The dough making was the best bit as far as they were concerned.

The dough:

*225g (8oz) strong flour*
*10g (½ oz) fresh yeast*
*1 teaspoon salt*
*55 ml (2 fl oz) milk*
*1 teaspoon sugar*
*2 small eggs*
*50g (2oz) butter*

The topping:

*700g (1½ lbs) tomatoes*
*1 dessertspoon oil*
*1 tablespoon chopped spring onions*
*1 tablespoon fresh basil*
*110g (4oz) Bel Paese cheese or Mozzarella (sliced)*

To make the dough, cream the yeast with the sugar. Add this to the milk, together with the well-beaten eggs. Sift the flour and the salt into a warmed basin. Now add to the first mixture and beat well. Have the butter ready creamed and then work into the paste. Cover and leave to rise for forty minutes. Meanwhile:

Peel the tomatoes, cut into quarters. Heat the oil and sauté the onions for 1-2 minutes. Add the tomatoes, herbs, a little salt and black pepper. Cook for 1-2 minutes, then cool slightly. Knead the dough until manageable. Place on a lightly floured pizza plate and pat to size. Scatter the tomato mixture on top, leaving any surplus liquid in the pan. Add the cheese, then leave to prove in a warm place for ten minutes. Bake in a hot oven 190-200 C (375-400F, gas mark 5-6) for twenty to thirty minutes. Serve piping hot.

# Canapés, Finger Food and Barbecues

**Over the Stream, Lulworth**

## Aloo Tikki – Sam Chalmers

For the strict vegetarians of North India, eggs are unacceptable, and although not mentioned in the recipe, you might like to add one or several, according to your judgement, to help bind the mixture. A simple, delightful barbecue alternative to burgers (cooked in olive oil in a paella pan on your "second" stove - what, you don't have one?) to keep vegetarians, like myself, from feeling neglected. And, by the way, in my experience, the meat-eaters grab them first.

Mix together (quantities you can guess):

*Mashed potatoes*
*Boiled peas*
*Cornflour, a little, to bind*
*Cumin powder*
*Chilli powder*
*Salt*

Make balls and flatten between palms. Fry on both sides until golden brown and crisp. Serve with mint chutney and coriander seeds. Keep the wine flowing and you won't have any complaints.

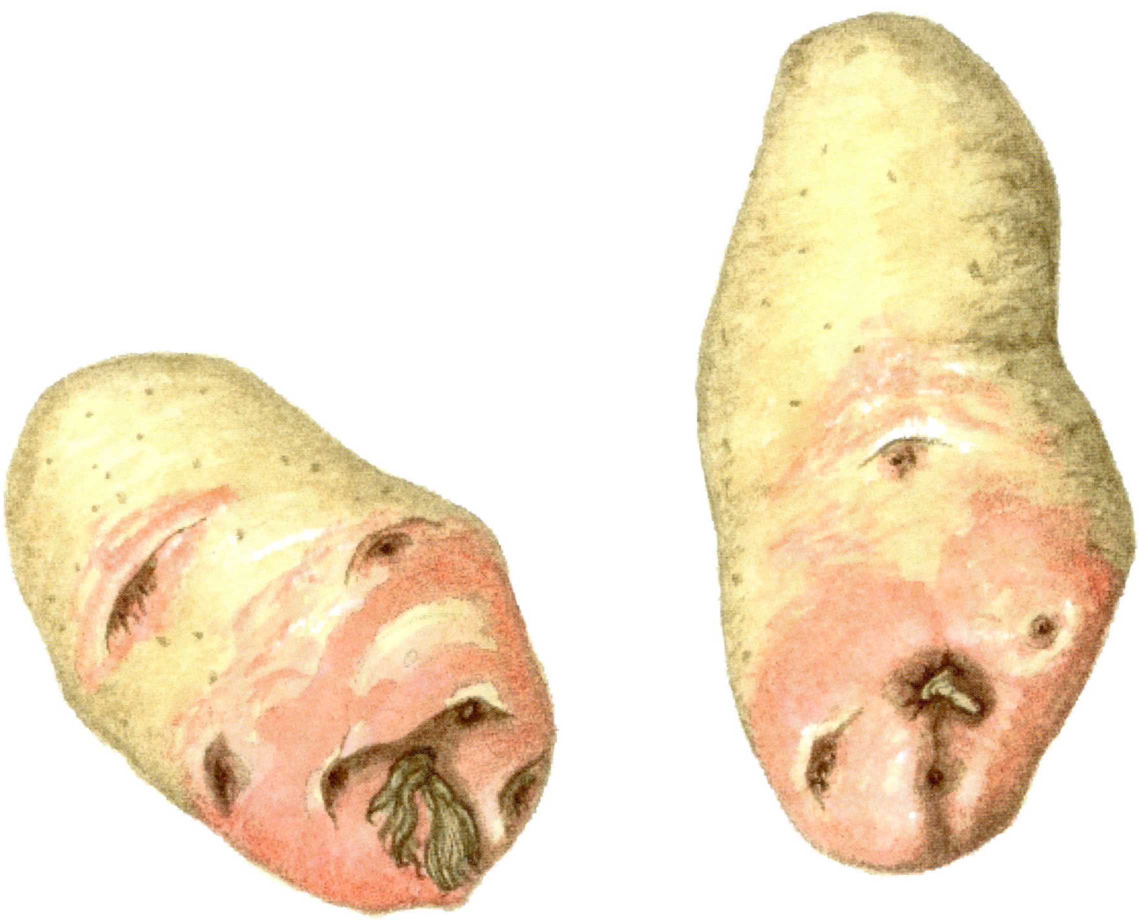

## Barbecued Scallops in Parma Ham and Basil – Sarah Pearce

I made these scallops for my mother's seventieth birthday lunch on the day of the total eclipse of the sun. Camera flashes were going off like a Mexican wave from Hambury Tout as I was trying to light the barbecue. Serves four.

*Virgin olive oil*
*Fresh basil*
*Pinch of salt*
*Ground black pepper*
*Juice of half a lemon*
*24 scallops, shells and corals removed*
*12 slices of Parma ham*

Up to twelve hours beforehand, marinate the scallops in olive oil, chopped basil, salt, sugar and pepper. (Chilli could also be used.) Add the lemon juice a couple of hours before you want to assemble the kebabs.

Cut the Parma ham into strips and wrap around each scallop. Thread them onto skewers (three per skewer, two skewers per person) using the skewer to secure the ham to the scallop. Cook them on the barbecue for about three minutes on each side. Scallops are always better undercooked.

Serve with green salad and new Jersey potatoes tossed in parsley butter, or minted butter.

## Jenny's Cheese Biscuits – Sarah Pearce

These are really good, and the recipe that I have been asked for most. Jenny Holsbert lives in Wareham, and, before her husband died, they would often come to help my mother when she gave a dinner party. Jenny would always appear with a large Tupperware box full of these wonderful nibbles. I have added a few extra flavours over the years. It is easy to make a mixed batch, and children love to help, though they can eat so many that you have to do it all over again!

Basic mixture:

*Equal quantities of butter, flour and grated cheddar cheese (usually 225g (8oz) of each)*
*Pinch of salt*
*Cayenne pepper to taste*

Put all the ingredients into a food processor and whizz until it forms a ball. Chill in the fridge for half-an-hour and then roll out on a floured surface. I press out the shapes using a lid from a Schwartz herb pot. Lay the shapes on a buttered baking sheet, brush with beaten egg or milk and sprinkle some with fennel seeds, some with poppy seeds, some with chopped rosemary and rather more with sesame seeds. Leave some plain. Bake in a medium oven until golden.

## Barbecue Recipes – Kevin Booker

### Home-made Beef burgers for six

*450g (1 lb) steak mince*
*50g (2oz) chopped onion*
*1 teaspoon chopped garlic*
*Salt and pepper*
*1 teaspoon Worcester sauce*
*1 teaspoon English mustard*
*2 slices white bread (no crusts) soaked in milk*
*1 egg*

Mix all together. Form into patties and cook over the barbecue.

### Chicken Kebabs

*Chicken fillets, cut into long strips, 1 tub natural yogurt, juice of 1 lemon, 1 spoon curry paste*

Mix together yogurt, lemon juice and paste. Marinate chicken strips for two hours. Soak bamboo skewers overnight in water. Snake chicken onto skewers and barbecue.

### Pork Ribs

*Pre-cooked ribs or belly pork, honey, chopped garlic*

Heat honey and garlic. Brush over ribs and grill on barbecue.

### Barbecue Sauce

*Brown sugar, vinegar, garlic, tomato ketchup, salt and pepper.*

Boil all together.

### Marinated Chicken

*Olive oil, mango chutney, chopped garlic, chopped shallots, chopped coriander, English mustard, paprika, salt and pepper.*

Mix all together, coat chicken and leave for four hours or overnight.

### Mango Dressing and Celebration Chicken

*Flesh of 1 ripe mango, zest and juice of 2 limes, salt and pepper, 275ml (½ pint) vegetable oil*

Blend mango, limes and seasoning in a food processor. Keep it running and add oil. Add to the above:

*Chopped cucumber, shallots, coriander. 1 tub natural yogurt, 275g (10oz) cooked chicken.*

## Mirza Ghassemi – Sam Chalmers

Aubergines are called Brinjal or Eggplants in Arabia and South Asia and are an underrated vegetable in the UK - purple isn't exactly a food colour, is it? However, they grow profusely in this region and provide an excellent foundation for non-meat dishes, especially hot dips using Arabic (Qubs) bread or Indian chapattis, rotis, parathas, or naan bread. Vary the quantities to suit.

*Aubergines*
*Eggs*
*Butter, olive oil*
*Garlic*
*Salt*
*Tomatoes*
*Tomato paste*
*Turmeric*
*Parsley*

Bake the aubergines in a pre-heated oven. Scrape out the pulp and discard the skin. Fry eggs in a non-stick pan, both sides, and cut into fine strips. Heat both butter and olive oil in a pan (here I have to mention the traditional French thick-bottomed "Marmite"-shaped stainless-steel pan with a lid with a steam hole - once used you will never use any other) – and sauté chopped garlic.
Add:

*Thinly sliced tomatoes.*
*Aubergine pulp and salt to taste.*
*Turmeric powder and tomato paste.*

Cook on a low heat for 15 minutes. Add the egg strips and mix carefully. Garnish the "mirza" with chopped parsley. Serve immediately, with the dipping bread of your choice.

This is a super cocktail party dip or buffet starter, and it must be eaten hot! By the way, Mirza Ghassemi is the name of the chap to whom the invention of the dish is attributed and he probably lived in what is now called the Lebanon.

## Grandmother's Remedies – Sally Lee

**Arthritis:** Wash and cook beetroot leaves in a very little water – do this quickly. Squeeze out the juice and drink hot or cold.

## Mrs Marshallsay's Cheese and Onion Bakes

Mrs Marshallsay's wonderful recipe is reproduced on the next page, just as she submitted it. For ease of use it is here reprinted in the same format as the rest.

...A favourite with young people.

*225g (8oz) plain flour*
*Pinch salt*
*175g (6oz) margarine in a hard block straight from the fridge*
*75g (3oz) grated cheese*
*Cold water to mix*
*3 level teaspoons Marmite (can be less)*
*6 teaspoons warm water (can be less)*
*350g (12oz) onions, finely chopped (important)*

*Swiss Roll tin 36 cm x 23 cm (14" x 9")*
*Fluted cutter 7cm (2 ¾") diameter*

Sieve flour and salt. Using coarse grater, grate margarine into flour. Add cheese and mix well together with a knife. Add the cold water, gradually mixing it in with your hand to feel the consistency, until you have a smooth but not too stiff dough. It should be a little softer than shortcrust, pliable but not sticky. Wrap in greaseproof paper and leave in a cool place for 15 minutes.

Meanwhile dissolve the Marmite in the hot water.

Roll out half the pastry a little larger than the tin and line the tin with it, pressing it well into the sides and base. Brush with the Marmite mixture and spread onions over it. Roll out and lay the other half of the pastry on the top, pressing edges together.

Mark into twelve pieces, and then, if desired, in half, to make twenty-four smaller pieces. With the fluted cutter, cut through the top layer of pastry in each square, (see illustration) and then brush the entire surface with remaining Marmite mixture.

Bake just above centre of fairly hot oven at 200 C (400 F, gas mark 6) for twenty minutes, then reduce heat to 190 C (375 F, gas mark 5) for a further fifteen to twenty minutes until golden.

Best eaten just warm.

Cheese and Onion Bakes a favourite with young people.

8 oz Plain flour, pinch salt.
6 oz margarine in a hard block straight from the fridge.
3 oz grated cheese, cold water to mix
3 level teas. Marmite (can be less)
6 teas warm water (can be less)
¾ lb onions, Finely chopped or grated. (important)
a Swiss Roll tin 14" x 9"
a 2¾" fluted cutter.

Sieve flour & salt. using coarse grater, grate margerine into flour, add cheese and mix well together with a knife. Add the cold water gradually, mixing it in with your hand to feel the consistency, until you have a smooth but not too stiff dough. It should be a little softer than shortcrust, pliable but not sticky. Wrap in greaseproof paper and leave in a cool place for 15 min. Meanwhile desolve the marmite in the hot water.
Roll out half the pastry a little larger than the tin and line the tin pressing it well into sides and base. Brush with the marmite and spread onions over it. Roll and lay the other on the top pressing edges together. Mark into 12 pieces, and then if desired each square in half,* With the fluted cutter, cut thru the top layer of pastry in each square see illustration? then brush entire surface with remaining marmite. Bake just above centre of fairly hot oven gas 6, 400F 200C for 20 min then reduce heat to gas 5, 375F 190C for further 15 to 20 min until golden. Best eaten just warm.

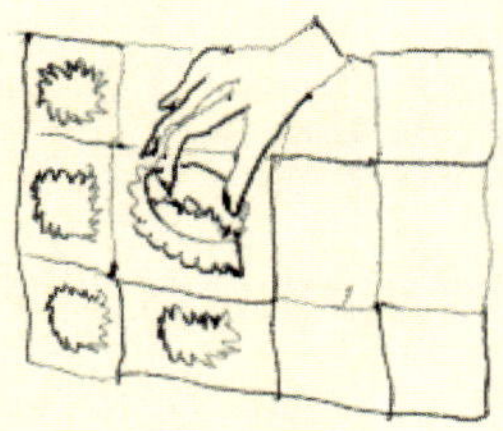

* to make 24 smaller pieces.

Mrs M Marshallsay
Carron
Colliers Lane
Wool Wareham
Dorset
BH20 6DJ

I'm very proud of that hand but dont include it if it dosent help.

## Grandmother's Remedies – Sally Lee

**Coughs:** cut a yellow turnip in slices or a large onion in rings. Cover with brown sugar and put plate over dish or basin. Leave overnight. The juice which you drain off will ease the cough.

## New Zealand Cheese Rollies – Anon, East Lulworth

*8 slices bread, crusts removed*
*1 egg, beaten*
*110g (4oz) cheddar cheese, finely grated*
*Salt, pepper, pinch dry mustard*
*50-75g (2-3oz) softened butter*
*8 rashers streaky bacon, rind removed*
*16 or 24 cocktail sticks*
*Sprigs parsley*

Butter the bread. Mix cheese and seasonings into beaten egg. Divide egg/cheese mixture between slices of bread. Spread over and roll each piece into a mini Swiss roll; then cut into two or three pieces. Cut each piece of bacon in half, or into three pieces, wrap round roll and secure with a cocktail stick. Place rollies on a greased baking tray, melt remaining butter, brush over each and bake at 200C (400F, gas mark 6) above centre oven until golden and crisp, approximately twenty minutes. The fat will cook out and quickly absorbs again when removed from the oven. Serve hot, warm or cold.

## Pappadam Prawn Roll – Sam Chalmers

Here is a recipe from South India, using small, about 10cm (4-inch) diameter, uncooked pappadams, or chapattis, if uncooked pappadams are difficult to find. Beth Barnes, an American calorie counter, said that what you eat standing up doesn't count. So, a delicious use of pappadams and prawns for stand-up, calorie-free, eating!

For the filling:

Put olive oil in a frying pan. Add, in the order given:

*Finely-chopped onions*
*Finely-chopped garlic and ginger*
*Finely-chopped green chillies, without seeds*
*Finely-chopped tomatoes*
*Finely-chopped prawns*
*Chilli and turmeric powder*
*Lime juice and salt*

Put aside to cool.

For the case:

Take the pappadams. Put a tablespoon of the filling in each pappadam and roll up. Seal ends with a beaten egg. Deep fry and serve with lime halves and cold beer. Make plenty - if you don't, they will be goa, goa, gone in no time.

## My Mother Said…

Use wooden chopping boards and scrub them thoroughly, daily.

# Drinks

The Stream, Lulworth Cove

## Quotations

I am certain the good Lord never intended grapes to be made into grape jelly.
*Attributed to Fiorello La Guardia in Bottled Wisdom, compiled and edited by Mark Pollman*

I have taken more out of alcohol than alcohol has taken out of me. *Winston Churchill*

Wine gives courage and makes man apt for passion. *Ovid*

Wine is an appropriate article for mankind, both for the healthy body and for the ailing man. *Attributed to Hippocrates*

I forget the name of the place; I forget the name of the girl; but the wine…was Chambertin. *Hilaire Belloc*

A feast of fat things, a feast of wine on the lees… *Isaiah 25:6*

Let us have wine and women, mirth and laughter, sermons and soda water the day after.
*Lord Byron from Don Juan, Canto 2, Stanza 178*

God in His goodness sent the grapes
To cheer both great and small;
Little fools will drink too much,
And great fools not at all. *Anon*

A man is never drunk if he can lie on the floor without holding on.
*Attributed to Joe E Lewis*

Go thy way, eat thy bread with joy, and drink thy wine with a merry heart, for God now accepteth thy works. *Ecclesiastes 9:7*

## Elderflower Cordial – Wendy Turney

Make a lot of this as it's very popular and you can freeze it.

*30 elderflower heads*
*1.5 litres (2½ pints) boiling water*
*1.8 kg (4 lbs) sugar*
*60g (2½ oz) citric acid or lemon*

Pour the boiling water onto all the ingredients. Stir night and day (morning and evening?) for five days. Strain through muslin into sterilised bottles and seal. Keep in fridge.

## Mahogany Pick-Me-Up – Sally Lee

Or should it be Put-Me-Down? You tell me! Mix:

*2 parts gin*
*1 part black treacle*

Beat well together.

## Refreshing Pearl Barley Water – Sally Lee

You can vary the proportion of oranges to lemons as you prefer.

*1 teacup pearl barley*
*6 oranges*
*2 lemons*
*Demerara sugar to taste*

Put pearl barley into boiling water and simmer for one hour. Squeeze fruit to separate juice. Strain barley water into another pan and add fruit skins and sugar to taste. Allow to stand until cool. Strain and add fruit juices.

## Mull Mixture – Sue Bartholomew

The Christmas time rehearsals of a choir of which I am a member have been known to end with a "little something" and a mince pie or two. One of our members produces this delicious, really orangey, mull, which, added to two bottles of red wine and heated gently, will warm the vocal chords of any (adult) chorister.

*6 large oranges, roughly cut into about 6 pieces*
*1.75 litres (3 pints) water*
*225g (8oz) granulated sugar*
*1 dessertspoon whole cloves*
*1 teaspoon cinnamon*
*1 teaspoon grated nutmeg*

Bring to the boil. Simmer for 30 minutes and strain. Add to *two bottles of red wine* and warm.

## Rum Punch – Sarah Pearce

On a starlit summer Lulworth evening a nutmeg scented rum punch is recommended. In winter, a rum punch taken at least twice a day is a happy cold cure. To make one rum punch you will need:

*2 tablespoons fresh lime juice (usually 1 lime)*
*4 tablespoons simple syrup*
*6 tablespoons golden rum*
*125ml (4 fl oz) water*
*3 ice cubes*
*Grated nutmeg*
*Sprig of fresh mint*

First, make some simple syrup by mixing 500g (1 lb) caster sugar with 450ml (¾ pint) cold water in a bowl. Stir until the sugar has dissolved. Pour into a bottle or jar to be kept in the fridge to make lots more rum punches.

Mix the lime juice, syrup, rum and water in a jug. Grate some fresh nutmeg into it. Pour over ice cubes in a tall glass and add a sprig of mint. Quaff!

## Granny Mees' Lemon Syrup – Tidal Favourites

As long as my mother lived she was requested to make Granny's lemon drink when any of the family came to stay. No modern lemonade can touch it for thirst quenching refreshingness.

*Juice and rind of 6 (unwaxed) lemons*
*10 cups (2.70kg, 6lbs) granulated or caster sugar*
*12 cups (3.25 litres, 5¾ pints) water*
*50g (2oz) citric acid*
*10g (½oz) epsom salts*
*25g (1oz) tartaric acid*

The last three ingredients can readily be bought at a good Chemist.

Put all together in a preserving pan and heat thoroughly. **Do not boil.** Strain and bottle. Dilute with iced water to taste, as for squash.

# First Courses

Lulworth Lobster

## Quotations

There is no sincerer love than the love of food. *George Bernard Shaw*

One cannot think well, love well, sleep well, if one has not dined well. *Virginia Woolf*

And do as adversaries do in law, strive mightily, but eat and drink as friends.
*William Shakespeare*

Talk of joy: there may be things better than beef stew and baked potatoes and home-made bread… there may be. *David Grayson, from Adventures in Contentment, 1907*

Our lives are not in the lap of the gods, but in the lap of our cooks.
*Lin Yutang, from The Importance of Living, 1937*

Kissing don't last: cookery do. *George Meredith*

One of the very nicest things about life is the way we must regularly stop whatever it is we are doing and devote our attention to eating.
*Luciano Pavarotti and William Wright, from Pavarotti, My Own Story*

When baking, follow directions. When cooking, go by your own taste. *Laiko Bahrs*

Hunger: one of few things that cannot be appeased with another solution.
*Irwin Van Grove*

It's difficult to think anything but pleasant thoughts when eating a homegrown tomato.
*Lewis Grizzard*

Forget love… I'd rather fall in chocolate! *Anon*

There is a lot more juice in grapefruit than meets the eye. *Anon*

If you wish to make an apple pie truly from scratch, you must first invent the universe.
*Carl Sagan*

## Artichoke Hearts and Prawns in Garlic Butter – Alan Smith

This recipe is, I fear, a total cheat: both in that it requires no cooking ability whatsoever, and also in that it was cribbed from the label of a can of artichoke hearts – albeit with the addition of prawns . . . It can be concocted at the last moment from store cupboard and freezer, and if cheats are not allowed to prosper there is always the hope that their guests may be allowed that privilege.

To serve two or three, depending on the appetite of the guests and the generosity of the host.

*1 tin artichoke hearts or bottoms*
*2 or 3 (depending on size) thawed prawns per heart*
*3 tablespoons olive oil*
*1 knob butter*
*3 tablespoons lemon juice*
*1 clove garlic, crushed*
*Salt and freshly ground black pepper to taste*

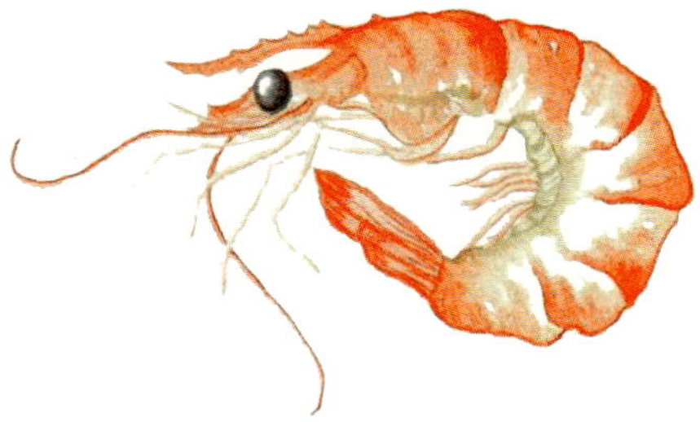

Drain the artichokes and place them in a saucepan with oil, butter, lemon juice, garlic and seasonings. Simmer for five minutes before adding prawns and warming through. Chopped parsley may be added; French bread is excellent for soaking up the sauce.

## Asparagus Mousse – Tidal Favourites

You can now buy imported asparagus almost all year round, and the little tips make an easy, quickly prepared mousse; not to be compared with eating the real thing in June, but good, even so. These quantities serve eight.

Blanch in boiling salted water until just tender:

*300g (11oz) asparagus tips (3 small supermarket packs)*

Meanwhile put into blender:

*125g (4½ oz) slightly salted butter (½ pack)*
*Juice of 1 small lemon*
*1 dessertspoon crème fraîche or double cream if preferred*
*(1 small packet of Boursin ail et fines herbes cream cheese is good, too, if liked)*
*1 snipped stem of spring onion, if liked*
*Pinch of sea salt, several grinds of black pepper, few drops of Tabasco*

With a draining spoon, transfer the just-cooked asparagus onto the ingredients in the blender, and process until smooth. If the mixture is too solid to process properly, add a few spoonfuls of the asparagus water, but not too much or the mousse will separate. Taste for seasoning. Pour into ramekins and put in the fridge to set.

Note: if you like a contrast in texture, crumble some crisp bacon over the top just before serving. This might be a good excuse for a weekend cooked breakfast, when the breakfast chef may be persuaded to grill you a few extra slices to keep for later…

## Carameled Grapefruit – Jane Pickton

Everybody knows this one…

Preheat grill

*One halved and sectioned grapefruit per person*
*Rum or Brandy*
*Dark brown or demerara sugar*

Pour on Rum/Brandy and top with brown/demerara sugar. Pop under the grill until it looks right.

## Champignons Gratinés – Margaret Whitehouse

Use quantities to suit.

*Mushrooms*
*Butter*
*White wine*
*Cream*
*Gruyere and Parmesan cheeses, grated*

Cut the stalks off the mushrooms and sauté in a little butter. Add a dash of white wine. Reduce liquid by half, add cream to three-quarters the depth of the mushrooms and reduce again, until it reaches coating consistency.

Place in serving dish, cover the top with the grated cheeses and grill until golden and bubbly.

## Cheese Dream Soufflé – Jilly Palmer

One of my mother's easy and delicious starters – it does not collapse! Serves four.

*425ml (3/4 pint) hot milk*
*50g (2oz) breadcrumbs*
*10g (1/2 oz) butter*
*110g (4oz) grated cheese*
*2 well beaten eggs*

Pour hot milk onto breadcrumbs and season with salt and pepper. Leave for twenty minutes. Add butter, cheese and eggs. Put into a buttered ovenproof dish and bake in a moderate oven on middle shelf.

Note: My mother (now in heaven, so out of reach of tiresome questions) omitted to say how long this should be cooked, but probably half an hour, or until risen, golden and smelling irresistible…

## Chicken Liver Paté – Valentine Simson

Feeds four for a light supper, or makes a good starter.

*25g (1oz) butter*
*225g (8oz) chicken livers*
*1/2 an onion, chopped*
*50g (2oz) breadcrumbs*
*3 tablespoons Sherry / cooking wine*

Melt the butter in a frying pan. Add chopped onion to soften and then add chicken livers. Cook until brown but not burnt! Remove from heat. Put into food processor with the breadcrumbs and sherry and blend until the mixture is smooth.

Turn into ramekin dishes and cover with clingfilm. Once cool can be kept in the fridge for three or four days. Can also be frozen for one month.

## Christmas Paté – Margaret Whitehouse

*450g (1 lb) belly of pork, as lean as possible*
*450g (1 lb) ox liver*
*175g (6oz) onion, peeled and chopped*
*1 large egg*
*1 level teaspoon tomato purée*
*1 level teaspoon mixed herbs*
*Salt and pepper*
*3 bay leaves*
*275ml (1/2 pint) aspic made from jelly powder*

Remove as much fat as possible; mince pork, liver and onions. Stir in egg, tomato purée and herbs until well blended. Add seasoning and mix in aspic. Put in paté dish with bay leaves on top and cover with foil. Cook in moderate oven at 160C (320F) for two hours. Leave to cool overnight.

## Continental Prawn Cocktail – Valentine Simson

*225g (8oz) frozen prawns, defrosted*
*225g (8oz) tin peaches*
*225g (8oz) tin pears*
*Black pepper*
*2 drops Tabasco*
*Lettuce*
*75ml (3oz) mayonnaise*
*55ml (2oz) tomato purée*
*1 teaspoon lemon juice*
*1 teaspoon icing sugar*

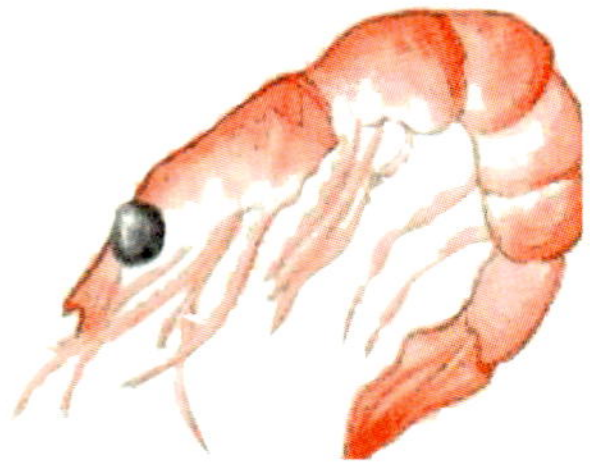

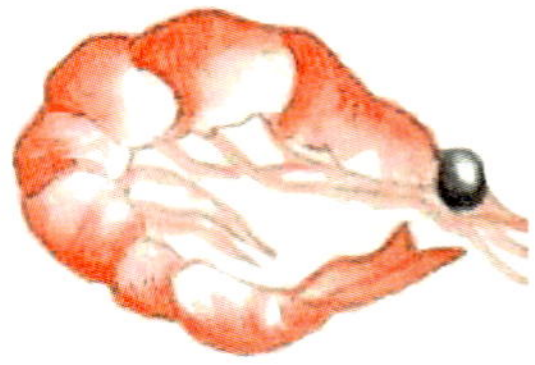

Drain peaches and pears; chop finely and put in a large dish with peeled and defrosted prawns. In a separate bowl mix mayonnaise, tomato purée, black pepper, lemon juice, Tabasco and icing sugar. Chop lettuce finely and place in serving dishes. Mix together the prawns, fruit and mayonnaise dressing and place on the bed of lettuce. Chill. Just before serving add a little red pepper or tomato to decorate. Serve with toast, or rolls and butter.

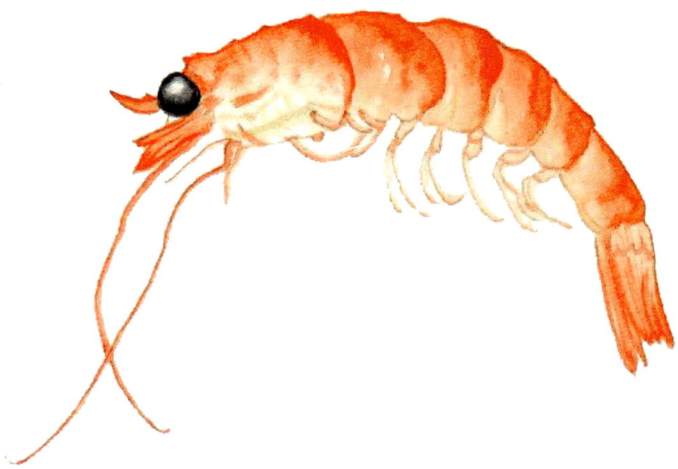

## Devilled Crab – Tidal Favourites

A useful starter for six to eight people; this is quick to do.

*2 dressed crabs*
*2 peeled, chopped garlic cloves*
*Olive oil to cover the bottom of the saucepan*
*1 teaspoon cayenne pepper or Tabasco*
*Pinch of sea salt, several grinds of black pepper*
*Handful of finely chopped parsley*

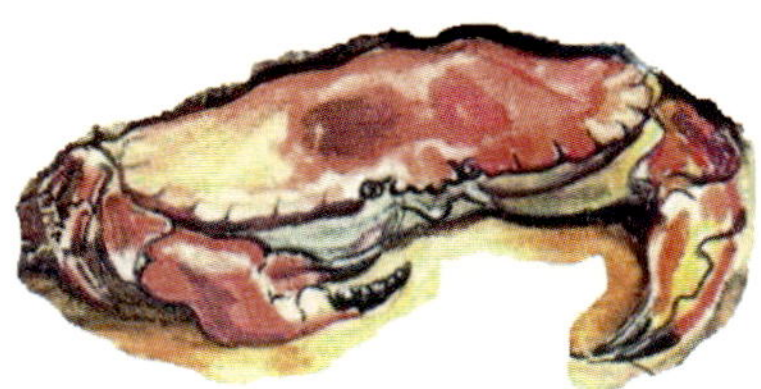

Gently sizzle the garlic in the oil; add all the other ingredients and heat through. Serve hot in ramekins to eat with a teaspoon. To accompany them, crackers with butter go well, but are not essential. If you have unexpected guests but no more crab, you can stretch the recipe by adding hard-boiled, chopped egg and a little cream. You may need to adjust the seasoning. For a crunchy topping, fry some slivered almonds until golden and serve separately for people to help themselves.

## Devil's Advocado – Alan Smith

Just because the devil has the best tunes, is that a reason for him not to be conceded the occasional ripe avocado?

Quantities **per person:**

*½ avocado, peeled and cubed*
*1 rasher streaky bacon*
*½ clove garlic, crushed*
*Dash of soy sauce*
*Cayenne pepper to taste*
*Salt and black pepper*

Fry the bacon with the garlic in the oil until the bacon is crisp. Remove and reserve. Just prior to serving, to the same oil add the avocado, soy sauce, pepper and seasonings: heat through. Serve with crispy bacon crumbled on top.

## Dorset Paté – Paulina Stretch

*175g (6oz) streaky bacon, rind removed*
*350g (12oz) pig liver, no gristle*
*175g (6oz) fatty pork*
*Salt, pepper*
*1 teaspoon anchovy essence (optional)*
*½ an apple*
*1 large garlic clove, crushed*
*1 dessertspoon cooking brandy (optional)*
*150ml (¼ pint) thick white sauce*
*1 bay leaf*

Place liver, pork, white sauce, apple, anchovy essence, garlic, salt, pepper and brandy in the liquidiser. Process to the desired consistency - this could be roughish or smooth according to preference. Pour into a straight-sided metal container, cover with bacon and bay leaf. Place the container in a roasting tin half filled with water and bake in the oven at 150C (300F, gas mark 2) for one and a half hours.

## Egg and Ham Mousse – Jilly Palmer

Vegetarians can omit the ham! Not only is this a useful starter, but it can also be served as a main course in an oiled ring with a central filling of chopped cucumber, celery, cherry tomatoes, etc. in vinaigrette. Serves six.

*225g (8oz) ham*
*110g (4oz) celery*
*3 hard-boiled eggs*
*2 tablespoons mayonnaise*
*1 tablespoon lemon juice*
*Small carton whipping cream*
*½ teaspoon celery salt*
*Chopped chives*
*2 packets gelatine dissolved in 150ml (¼ pint) stock*
*2 egg whites*

Combine all ingredients, chopped finely. Whisk cream, add lemon juice and stir into mixture. Add dissolved gelatine. Whisk egg whites and fold into mixture.

Oil 6 cocotte or ramekin dishes and divide the mixture between them. Leave to set overnight. Turn out and garnish with celery leaves. Serve with brown bread and butter.

## Grapefruit and Seafood Cocktail – Jilly Palmer

This is a good starter to serve before a rather rich main course. Serves four.

*2 grapefruit*
*4 cups cooked shrimp, prawn, lobster, crab – or a mixture of seafood*
*French dressing*
*4 drops Tabasco*
*2 drops Angostura*

Halve grapefruit and remove sections of the fruit. Scoop out pith and membranes. Add grapefruit sections to the seafood mixture with French dressing to taste, with the Tabasco and Angostura (if available). Fill grapefruit halves with the mixture. Sprinkle with chopped parsley and serve chilled.

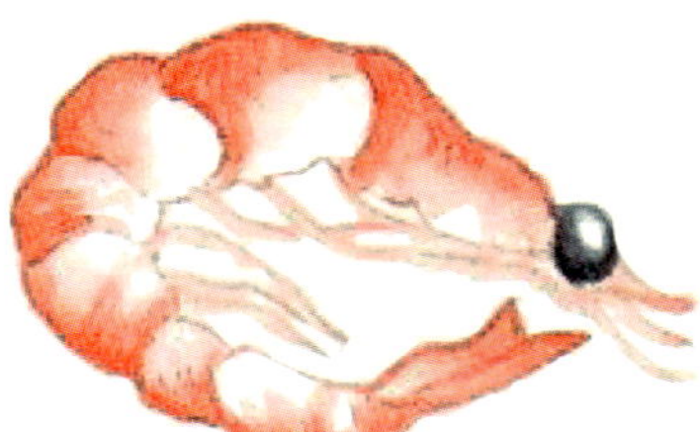

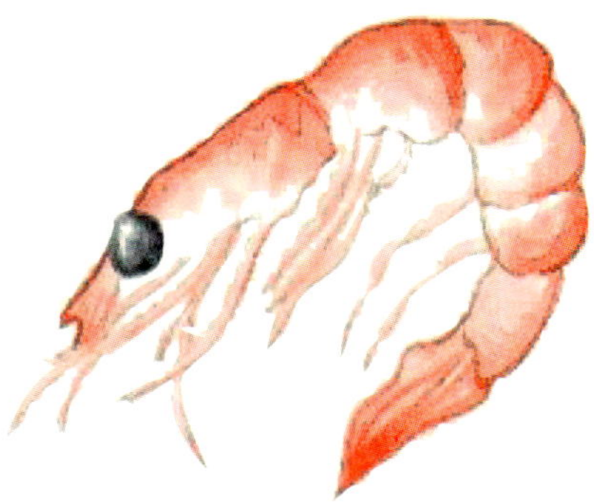

## My Mother Said…

Work quickly at all times – you'll never get through it otherwise!

## Haddock and Egg in Aspic – Anne Dickson

Serves eight to ten.

*700g (1½ lb) smoked haddock*
*7 eggs*
*425ml (¾ pint) double cream*
*275ml (½ pint) aspic*
*1-2 teaspoons Anchovy Sauce*
*1-2 teaspoons Harvey Sauce*
*1-2 teaspoons Worcester Sauce*
*Black pepper*

Hard-boil eggs and make aspic. Poach haddock. (Just pour boiling water over haddock fillets to cover and leave covered until cold). Separate egg yolks and whites. Sieve yolks and add the three sauces. Add seven tablespoons of liquid aspic. Put remaining aspic in fridge. To mixture add cream slowly. Chop egg whites and flake haddock: add to mixture. Season with pepper. Put in 1.2 litre- (2-pint)-sized pudding basin. Set in fridge for several hours – perhaps overnight. Garnish with remaining aspic (chopped), parsley and (if liked) watercress.

## Jonathan's Starter – Anne Watts

Jonathan is my son-in-law, and it was he who devised and gave me this unusual starter. Serves six to eight.

*1 tub cream cheese, minimum 250g (9oz)*
*3 spring onions, very finely chopped*
*3 gherkins, very finely chopped*
*15 slices salami of choice, standard size*

Mix together the first three ingredients and season to taste. Spread the cream cheese mixture on the salami and repeat until you have five layers. Repeat twice more. Wrap in cling film and chill for several hours; it needs to be well chilled before cutting. Cut into eight wedges just before serving. Dress with light salad garnish and serve with thin slices of brown bread.

## Marinated Kipper Fillets – Jilly Palmer

This is a delicious and useful first course, as it can be prepared well in advance. Serves four.

*1 packet boned kipper fillets*
*1 small onion*
*1 bay leaf*

Separate kipper fillets and pull away the silvery skin from the back of each. Arrange the fillets in a shallow serving dish. Peel and slice the onion and place over the top with the bay leaf.

*Salt and freshly milled pepper*
*1 level teaspoon caster sugar*
*3 tablespoons wine vinegar*
*4 tablespoons olive oil*

Combine salt, pepper, sugar and vinegar for the marinade. Stir to dissolve the seasonings and add the oil. Mix and pour over the kipper fillets. Leave for several hours or overnight to marinate, turning the fillets occasionally. Lift the fillets from the marinade and serve with brown bread and butter.

## Marinated Herrings in Sour Cream – Geoffrey Donald

This is a favourite starter in the USA. Marinated herring (with or without sour cream) can be bought ready prepared from most delicatessens, which saves much fiddling around with homemade marinades and herbs. This recipe will much improve them by adding extra exciting tastes. Make sure you buy the kind with thin filleted strips of herring flesh already removed from the bone and marinated, rather than the whole fish sometimes found in tins.
Serves four to six as a starter.

*450g (1lb) prepared marinated herring*
*A small onion, or part of a larger one*
*A small bunch of spring onions*
*A large cooking apple*
*300ml (10 fl oz) carton soured cream*
*Juice of one lemon*
*2 teaspoons sugar*

If not already so, cut the herring fillets into inch squares, and arrange neatly in a layer at the bottom of a large shallow serving dish. Cover with any of the sour cream marinade that may have come with them.
Finely chop the onion and place in a mixing bowl. Top and tail the spring onions; slice into quarter inch lengths, reserving some of the green leaf parts. Add the rest to the bowl. Pour in the sour cream, add the lemon juice and sugar and mix thoroughly. It may be necessary to adjust the taste between the lemon and sugar a little. Cut the apple, top to bottom, into eight sections; peel and de-core each, and slice and chop into small pieces. Add these to the bowl and fold in before they start to turn brown. Pour the mixture evenly over the herrings and leave in a cool place for an hour or so. If you put it in the refrigerator don't allow it to get too cold!
Just before bringing the dish to the table, garnish it with the green onion tops and perhaps a sprinkling of chopped parsley.

## Grandmother's Remedies – Sally Lee

**For a Bad Bruise:** Be like Jack and Jill and cover it with vinegar and brown paper.

## Mushrooms and Prawns in Garlic Butter – Alan Smith

Mushrooms in garlic butter is a well-known starter; likewise prawns in the same liquid. Both have the advantage of utter simplicity of preparation. While deciding between the two some ten minutes before guests were due to arrive, I was struck by a flash of gastronomic inspiration of the sort usually granted only to real cooks or those contemplating telephoning the local takeaway: I combined the two. Judge for yourselves before dialling.

Quantities are **per person:**

*Two open field mushrooms*
*Six cooked, peeled prawns*
*A knob of butter*
*½ clove of garlic, crushed*
*Salt and pepper to taste*
*A dash of sherry or Madeira*

Gently cook the mushrooms in the butter, garlic, sherry and seasonings. When they are soft add the prawns, heat through and serve.

On a slice of warm toast, this can also serve as a lunchtime snack. So can the sherry.

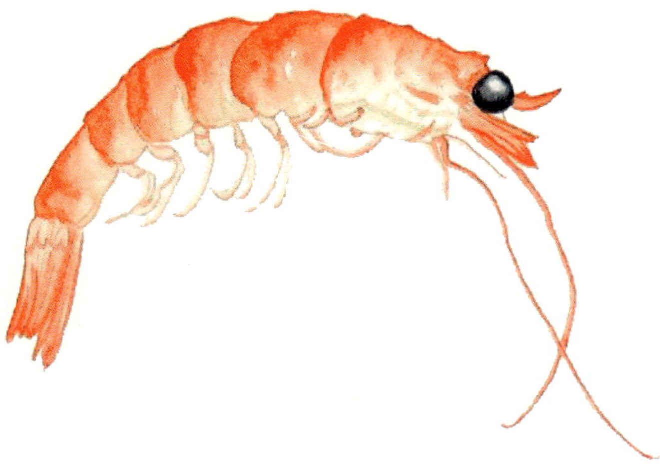

## Prawns and Mushrooms En Cocotte – Jilly Palmer

This is a useful starter as it is hot, but can be prepared beforehand, and just popped into the oven for ten – fifteen minutes while you enjoy an aperitif. Can be followed by a cold main course and pudding – maybe after a visit to the theatre or the local pantomime? Serves six.

*225g (½ lb) sliced mushrooms*
*225g (½ lb) prawns*
*275ml (½ pint) good white sauce with some white wine and the juice of the mushrooms added*

Stir mushrooms and prawns into the white sauce. Spoon into ramekins. Sprinkle with breadcrumbs or grated cheese and bake for ten to fifteen minutes in a hot oven until brown and crisp on top.

## Pawpaw and Prawn Crunch – Tidal Favourites

Leave out the shellfish for those allergic to them; you will still have an unusual and attractive starter, which is easy to do in advance. Quantities are given per person.

*$1/3^{rd}$ of a Pawpaw*
*3 or 4 prawns or shrimps*
*A few chunks of melon (or orange or anything else in the fruit bowl)*
*Lemon juice*
*Sesame or Walnut oil*
*Black pepper*
*½ a slice of grilled crumbled bacon, or toasted almonds, for crunch*

Divide the fruit and shellfish between the ramekins you'll serve them in, and squeeze a few drops of lemon juice over them. Follow this with black pepper and a dessertspoon of walnut or sesame oil. Finally, crumble crisp bacon or toasted almonds over the top. Refrigerate until needed.

## Prawns in Aspic – Sheila Rothwell

An easy starter when you are short of time. Serves four.

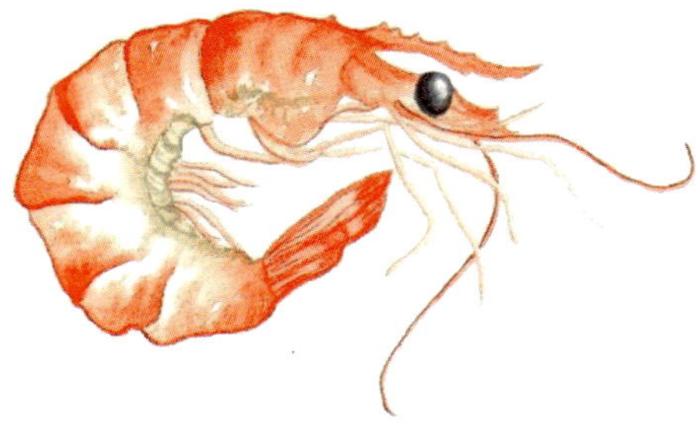

*225/350g (½ / ¾ lb) prawns*
*1 tin consommé (about 300ml or 10½ oz)*
*30ml (1 fl oz) water*
*25g (1oz) gelatine*
*Juice of half a lemon*
*4 tablespoons sherry*

Dissolve gelatine in water. Put consommé in a serving bowl with lemon juice and sherry, add gelatine liquid and as many prawns as you need. Set in fridge.

## Salmon Mousse – Val Blandamer

This is a quick and easy recipe and tastes delicious – a great favourite and an excellent starter for any dinner party.

*2 x 210g tins red salmon*
*1 x 210g tin pink salmon*
*6 tablespoons water*
*6 tablespoons wine vinegar*
*2 packets gelatine*
*4 sticks celery, roughly chopped*
*1 level tablespoon sugar*
*1½ level tablespoons capers*
*1½ level teaspoons dry mustard*
*Salt and pepper*
*420ml (¾ pint) double cream*
*Watercress for garnish*

Drain salmon, reserve juice, discard dark skin and bones. Warm water and vinegar in a pan, add gelatine and stir until dissolved. Put chopped celery in a food processor; add gelatine mix and blend until smooth. Add salmon, juice, capers, mustard, salt and pepper and blend until smooth. Whip cream until doubled in bulk but not stiff and fold into prepared salmon mixture.

Pour into a 3-pint ring or fish mould; chill until set. Dip mould in hot water and turn Mousse on to a serving plate and garnish with watercress.

## Sardine Paté – Anne Dickson

*2 tins sardines in oil (drained)*
*150g (5oz) Philadelphia cheese*
*6 very thin slices of onion*
*10 stoned black olives (optional)*
*6 sprigs parsley*
*3 tablespoons lemon juice*
*Tabasco in generous dashes*
*Salt and pepper*

Put all ingredients into a food processor and purée. Pile into serving dishes and cover with cling film. Keeps well in fridge, but remove an hour or two before serving.

For a novelty instead of a serving dish they look very nice served in a scooped out lemon.

## Smoked Haddock Paté – Anne Watts

Undyed smoked haddock is preferable, if you can get it. Serves six.

*350g (12oz) smoked haddock*
*50g (2oz) butter*
*200g (7oz) double cream*
*2 teaspoons lemon juice*
*1 teaspoon Worcester sauce*
*Pepper and cayenne pepper to taste*
*50g (2oz) melted butter for topping*

Poach the haddock for ten minutes, then drain, bone and flake. Mix the prepared haddock with the butter and liquidize. Fold in stiffly whipped cream, season and add lemon juice and Worcester sauce. Put into dish and pour melted butter over. Put in the fridge to set.

## Smoked Mackerel and Cottage Cheese Paté – Xenia Johnston

Serves six.

*350g (12oz) smoked mackerel*
*110g (4oz) cottage cheese*
*150g (5oz) butter*
*2 tablespoons creamed horseradish*
*Juice of half a lemon*
*3 tablespoons single cream*
*Salt and freshly milled pepper*

Mash the flesh of the fish after having removed the skin and bones. Add the cottage cheese, 75g (3oz) of the melted butter and the rest of the ingredients. Mix well. For a very smooth paté, blend in the liquidiser. Put into an oval dish or a foil freezer dish. Melt the remaining butter and pour over the flattened surface of the paté. Place in the refrigerator for the butter to set. Serve with toast or a small salad.

Note: This freezes well.

## Smoked Salmon Roulade – Jean Bourgeois

One great advantage of this starter is that it can be prepared well in advance of the party, which is just as well, because it takes a little time to make. Another is that it looks and tastes wonderful and can be served to Coeliacs. Serves six to eight.

For the Roulade:

*350g (12oz) cod fillet*
*275ml (½ pint) slightly salted water (or fish stock if you have it)*
*1 tablespoon chopped fresh dill*
*5 eggs, separated*
*1 ripe avocado, stoned and peeled*
*Salt and black pepper*

Line a Swiss roll tin approximately 32 x 23 cm (13 x 9 inches) with bakewell paper. Poach the cod fillet in fish stock until tender (for 3 minutes in microwave). Drain thoroughly and check for bones. Mash with the avocado. The fish should still have some texture. Season and beat in chopped dill and egg yolks (one at a time). Whisk the egg whites until stiff, but not dry. Fold into the fish mixture. Pour into the tin and bake (2nd shelf down) at 82C (180F) for 17 minutes until firm on top, but spongy to touch. Turn out onto a clean piece of baking parchment and lay a damp tea towel over the lining paper. Leave to cool for 1 hour. Remove tea towel and peel off paper. While the roulade cools, have a cup of coffee and make the filling:

*3 tablespoons thick mayonnaise (home made or use Helman's regular, not "lite")*
*1 tablespoon red lumpfish roe (use whole jar)*
*100g (4oz) thinly sliced smoked salmon*

Mix the mayonnaise with the lumpfish roe and season to taste. Spread over the roulade and lay the smoked salmon on top. Roll up and sprinkle with parsley. Let it settle for a bit before cutting. Ideally the dish should be used the same day as it is made, but any leftovers will make a delicious lunch the next day. It doesn't freeze.

## Stir-fried Prawns with Mange-touts – Jilly Palmer

This is best with tiger prawns for a treat, but smaller ones are fine. Serves four.

*16 uncooked tiger prawn tails or 225g (8oz) prawns*
*1 tablespoon vegetable oil*
*2 chopped spring onions*
*2 teaspoons grated fresh ginger*
*1 fresh green chilli, de-seeded and finely chopped*
*2 tablespoons light soy sauce*
*2 teaspoons tomato paste*
*1 tablespoon dry sherry*
*150g (5oz) mange-touts, trimmed*
*Sesame seeds and chopped fresh coriander, to garnish*

Rinse prawns with shells on and pat dry with kitchen paper. Heat oil and stir fry onions, ginger and chilli for one minute. Add prawns and stir fry for another minute. Tiger prawns will turn pink. Add soy sauce, tomato paste and sherry and cook for a further three minutes, stirring occasionally. Serve immediately garnished with sesame seeds, accompanied by boiled rice sprinkled with fresh coriander.

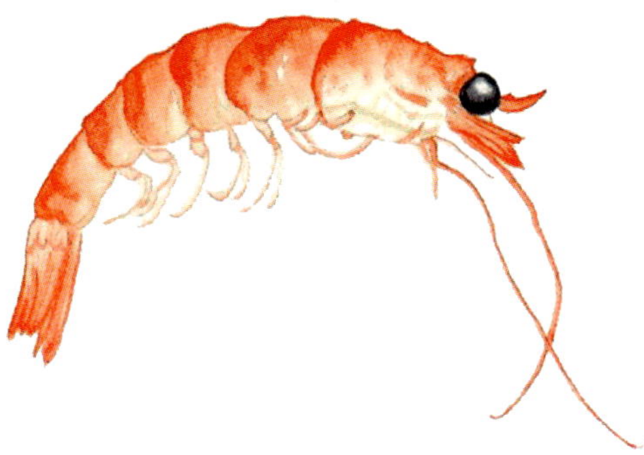

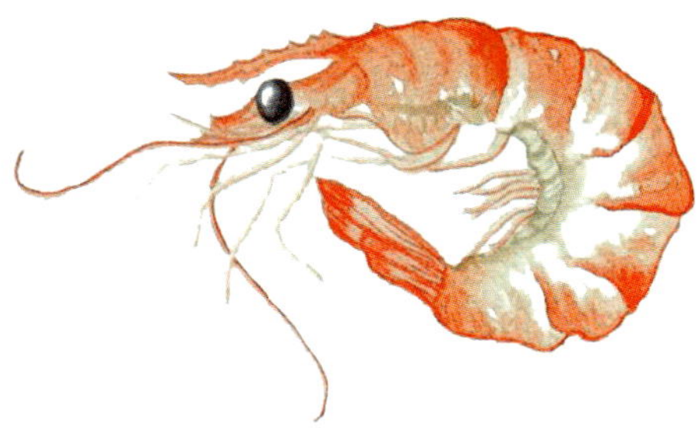

## Tuna Appetiser – Anne Watts

Allow a half to one egg per person, depending on appetites! Serves six to eight.

*Endive or lettuce*
*3 or 4 tomatoes, peeled*
*Hard-boiled eggs*
*275ml (½ pint) mayonnaise*
*½ cup flaked tuna*
*1 teaspoon lemon juice*
*Seasoning*
*Olives, if wished*

Arrange a little endive or shredded lettuce on individual plates. Place a thick slice of peeled tomato on the lettuce and cover with half a hard-boiled egg, round side up. Add flaked tuna to mayonnaise with lemon juice and seasonings. Cover egg with tuna mayonnaise. Garnish with olives and a sprinkle of paprika if wished.

## Tsatsiki – Tidal Favourites

In typical holiday fashion we came across this dish in a magical Corfiot taverna perched on the edge of an impossibly beautiful bay. It was served with good local bread, but the kindly proprietors supplied me with wedges of tomato as a gluten-free base, as I cannot eat bread. It was delicious with both, and makes as good an addition to salads as it does a starter or dip. This is my analysis of the ingredients: the combination of mild and creamy Greek yogurt, innocent cucumber and raw garlic is truly wicked.

*1 cucumber*
*1 500g pot of Greek yogurt*
*1 large clove of garlic (or more, Greek-style)*
*Squeeze of lemon juice*
*1 teaspoon of sugar*
*Salt and pepper*
*Dash of Tabasco*

Greek cucumbers are wonderful: so are the ones my husband grows. His grow like Topsy, which is what they're called; they are small, sweet and have no woody pips or bitter skin. Demand the best from your local cucumber centre!

Chop the cucumber and garlic very very fine. You can do this with a food processor, but don't purée it; there should still be some discernible chunks. Mix in all the rest of the ingredients. Cover with clingfilm and chill if you are not serving it immediately.

## Two Bachelor Starters

Two friends of ours, frequent visitors to Lulworth, dashed these elegant, colourful starters off for us on the back of an envelope. Both men are renowned for their dinner parties, although it's a mystery how they have time to cook for them, as Gareth Jones is Director of Music at The Dragon School, Oxford, and Stephen Wilkinson, also a superb pianist, is Head of Maths at Canford School. I couldn't resist reproducing Gareth's original, which he was still explaining and illustrating as he rushed for his car.

### Gareth's Starter

A great combination of tastes…

*Goat's cheese, usually Crottin or Bûche*
*Red and yellow peppers, cut in quite big pieces*
*Olive oil*
*Cooked plain beetroot, not in vinegar*
*Balsamic vinegar*

Roast the peppers in olive oil, allowing them to caramelise a bit. Set aside to cool, but do not peel. Reserve the oil and juices for the dressing. Cut the beetroot into wedges. Arrange the cold roasted peppers and the beetroot in a star on each plate, leaving space in the middle for the cheese.

When you are nearly ready to serve, heat your grill to very hot, while you cut the Crottin cheeses in half or slice the Bûche into thick pieces like a Swiss roll.

Grill the cheese pieces under very high heat, watching all the time, until they are nicely browning. Place them in the middle of your stars and drizzle the roast pepper oil and balsamic vinegar over the vegetables.

Alternatively, you can toss the cold vegetables with some salad greens in the peppers' oil and balsamic vinegar and serve as a salad to accompany the hot grilled cheeses.

## Gareth's Original

A great combination of tastes

Grilled goats cheese — very hot grill until browning (Watch all the time) usually crottin or Bûche.

(crottin cut in half – Bûche a slice) like Swiss roll

Roasted peppers (quite big pieces) Red & yellow (not green) in olive oil.

Beetroot – not in vinegar cut in wedges.

Arrange either as a salad with greens

or as a star

Dressing

use oil from peppers + balsamic

no dressing for 'star' just pan oil + balsamic vinegar

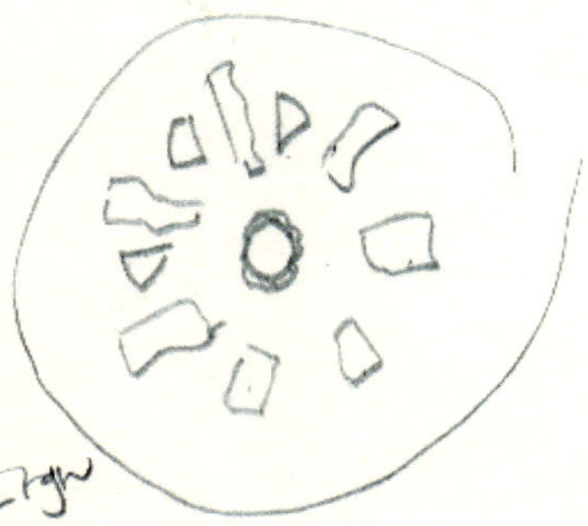

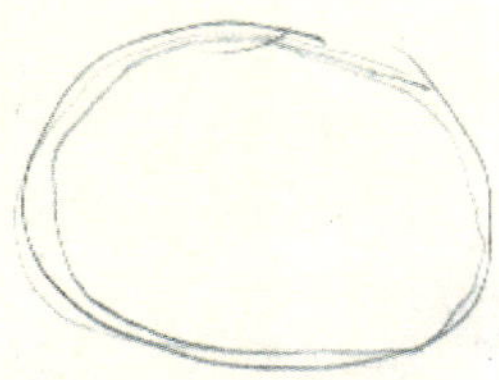

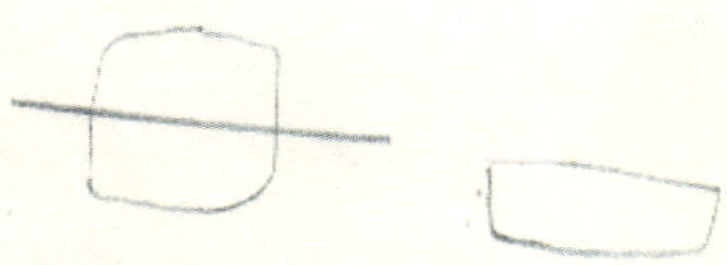

Buche cut in ½ slices per person.

## Silky Wilky's Raw Sardine and Roast Vegetable Starter

Even unadventurous eaters can't believe how wonderful this simple combination is. The texture of the fish cuts through the juiciness of the roast vegetables… a real appetiser. Serves four.

*4 rondelles of French bread*
*Olive oil*
*1 red pepper*
*1 yellow pepper and/or any other vegetable suitable for roasting*
*2 shallots*
*4 large sardines, very fresh*
*Lemon or lime juice with a little sugar and tarragon, for the marinade*
*Sea salt and black pepper*

Fillet the sardines. (This is easy with a sharp knife.) Marinate them in the lemon juice, sugar, tarragon, and salt and pepper mixture in the fridge for at least an hour or over night.

Pre-heat the oven to 200C (400F). Cut out the centres of the peppers and cut the flesh into fat strips. Skin the shallots. Put the peppers and shallots in a baking dish with some olive oil sprinkled on top and put in the hot oven.

Soak the bread in olive oil so both sides are covered completely. Ten minutes after starting the peppers put in the bread. After another thirty minutes, take everything out and allow to cool.

Just before serving, arrange the croûtons on plates, with the peppers and shallots scattered negligently over them. Place the sardine fillets on each and pour any spare oil from the cooking on top.

## Vonnie's Cold Cheese Soufflé – Jilly Palmer

As a new army wife in Benghazi I plucked up courage to ask the Colonel's wife to give me this recipe. She gladly gave it to me, and remained a kind friend for life, and a good example for me when I eventually took her place.

*275ml (½ pint) good white sauce*
*1 egg yolk*
*75g (3oz) Gruyere cheese*
*Salt, pepper, mustard*
*1 packet gelatine*
*2-3 tablespoons stock*
*Squeeze of lemon*
*1 carton whipping cream*
*3 egg whites*

Beat egg yolk into cooled sauce. Add cheese and seasoning. Dissolve gelatine in hot stock. Add to mixture with lemon juice. When cool fold in whipped cream and beaten egg whites. Pour into a soufflé dish with oiled jar in the middle (or a ring mould). When set remove jam jar and fill the middle with watercress. Garnish with tomatoes.

## Warm Spinach Bacon and Chicken Salad – Doreen Milligan

Good for a starter, but this will expand to make a main course with more chicken.

*2 skinless chicken breasts*
*Salt, pepper, lemon juice and Tabasco*
*500g (1 lb 2oz) tiny spinach leaves, washed*
*1 large avocado*
*1 medium sweet red onion*
*110g (4oz) cherry tomatoes, quartered*
*110g (4oz) smoked streaky bacon, de-rinded and diced*
*2 tablespoons olive oil*

Dressing:

*2 tablespoons wine vinegar*
*3 tablespoons olive oil*
*3 teaspoons tomato ketchup*
*½ teaspoon sugar*
*Salt, pepper, lemon juice and Tabasco*

Dice and season chicken breasts. Tear spinach into salad bowl. Slice onion; skin and dice avocado; add to bowl with tomatoes. Mix dressing and season to taste. (It needs to be quite sharp to balance the extra oil with the bacon and chicken.) Cook the bacon in a heavy frying pan until crisp. Remove bacon, leaving the fat in the pan; add olive oil to pan and cook chicken over high heat, turning to cook it through. Scatter, with the bacon, over the salad. Pour the dressing into the pan; stir and heat through. Pour over the salad, toss well and serve at once.

## Rescuing Saucy Disasters

There is a famous story about a quick-thinking Edwardian hostess, who said, as the maid tripped on a rug and deposited the Christmas turkey onto the floor: "Never mind, Mary. Just take it back to the kitchen and bring in *the other one...*"

Sleight of hand can often rescue a mistake, along with a good helping of aplomb.

It is all too easy to pour too much oil into a whirring mayonnaise, so that the egg liaison does not hold, and it splits. Pour the whole lot into a jug, and start again with another egg, with a little sugar and mustard, in the blender. Whizz away, and then slowly pour the curdled mixture into it, as if it were straight oil. Stop when it's good and thick.

A similar trick works with Hollandaise if you've added too much butter. Put another egg yolk into a clean bowl, with a squeeze more lemon juice, and slowly add the split mixture while stirring over simmering water.

Before making real custard, fill a washing up bowl with cold water. If the custard starts to split, pop the saucepan into the cold water, stirring madly, while it cools and recovers.

Lumpy gravy or white sauce can be pushed through a metal sieve if all else fails, but can usually be avoided by using my mother's infallible method for making a thickened sauce. Make your roux (butter, or the fat and glazes in the roasting pan, and flour or corn flour) loose and bubbly, rather than stiff. Pour your liquid, cold, over it all at once, and stir like crazy, over heat. A flat-bottomed slotted wooden implement is ideal for this. Keep stirring until it is smooth and thick and glossy, and then add your flavourings and seasonings. You can thin it with more liquid at this stage, if need be.

Another method is useful for making chicken gravy, when the juices in the roasting pan are rather watery. In a large jug, mix two or three heaped spoonfuls of corn flour, or gluten-free flour, with a little cold water, until smooth and creamy. Add water or cold stock until the jug is nearly full. Stir well. Pour this into the roasting pan and stir and scrape all the lovely glazes from the bottom of the pan while heating. When thick and glossy, add seasonings and flavourings. Sherry is good here. Better still, while you are mixing up the flour and liquid, have a young assistant (any age young will do) pour some wine into the roasting pan, stirring and boiling off the alcohol until you are ready to slosh in the jug full.

## My Mother Said...

What the eye doth not see, the heart doth not grieve over.

Of any minor disaster: a blind man would be glad to see it.

Le monde tourne encore...

# Fish

Shell Fish

## Chilean Scallops – The Weld Arms, East Lulworth

Quantities are given for one serving.

*4 mushrooms*
*3 scallops*
*3 rashers streaky bacon*
*Lime, lemon and black pepper*
*50g (2oz) rice*
*Seasoning*

Wrap scallops in bacon and skewer them alternately with the mushrooms until a long skewer is full. Sprinkle lime and lemon over and season with black pepper. Leave for one hour. Make the buerre blanc sauce:

*12 shallots (finely chopped)*
*225g (8oz) very cold diced butter*
*150ml (¼ pint) dry white wine*
*1 tablespoon crème fraîche*

Put shallots and wine in saucepan and bring to boil over moderate heat. Reduce to one third. Add the butter, whisking continuously to blend it in. Whisk in the crème fraîche. As soon as the sauce has turned white add salt and pepper to taste. Cook the rice in water with a little oil and salt. When cooked, drain and wash off in hot water and dress onto plate. Meanwhile, lightly grill the scallops (don't overcook) and serve on the bed of rice. Pour the butter sauce over. Garnish with cucumber, lemon and parsley.

## Cod with Spiced Red Lentils - Jennifer Halsall

I found this in a magazine years ago whilst waiting in the Doctor's Surgery. It is one of our favourite fish dishes; unusual and full of flavour. It can be made ahead of time.

*175g (6oz) red lentils*
*¼ teaspoon turmeric*
*600ml (1 pint) fish stock (cube) or water*
*1 tablespoon oil*
*1½ teaspoons cumin seed*
*1 tablespoon chopped fresh root ginger*
*½ teaspoon cayenne*
*Juice of ½ lemon*
*4 tablespoon fresh coriander or parsley, chopped (can use dried)*
*450g (1 lb) fresh cod or any white fish, skinned and cut into 5cm (2") pieces*
*Sprigs of coriander and lemon wedges to serve*

Place lentils in saucepan with turmeric and stock and simmer, covered, for about twenty minutes. Remove from heat and add salt to taste. In a small pan heat the oil, add the cumin seeds and when they begin to pop and splutter add ginger, cayenne, lemon and two teaspoons chopped coriander or parsley. Stir and fry for thirty seconds. Add to lentils. Lay pieces of the fish on top of the lentils, cover and cook gently until the fish is cooked, about ten minutes. Transfer to warm serving dish and sprinkle with remaining coriander. Serve with rice and a side salad.

## Coquilles St Jacques Dieppoise – Tidal Favourites

This is a dinner party dish and takes some time to make, but your friends will love it. Fresh scallops are ideal; however, we don't all live by the sea, and frozen are fine.

*1 large pack of frozen scallops or equivalent fresh ones (allow 2-3 per person)*
*1 large pack of frozen prawns or shrimps*
*1 bottle of dry white wine (or enough to cover the shellfish)*
*A handful of sea salt, a bay leaf, a dash of Tabasco, several grinds of black pepper*
*Dollop of double cream*
*About 250g (8oz) or so of strong grated cheddar*

Put the scallops and prawns into a large saucepan and cover with the wine. Bring to simmer and take off the heat the second the scallops are just cooked and tender. This is likely to be four or five minutes from simmer point. Test with a fork; they toughen if overcooked. Remove the shellfish with a draining spoon and either set aside (in fridge) or put into their final serving dishes. Traditionally they are served in their own shells but ovenproof 'shells', ramekins or a large baking dish that goes under the grill are equally good. Let the cooking liquor cool while you get on with another course, but don't let the cat anywhere near the kitchen…

For the next stage, make a roux with:

*About ¼ pack of butter*
*Enough flour or cornflour to make a loose bubbly roux*

Melt the butter in a saucepan and add the flour; pour half the cooled shellfish liquor into the roux all at once and stir hard over heat until it thickens. Add more liquor if it is too thick. (The remainder makes a good base for a fish stock, and could be frozen for future use.) When smooth and glossy add a dollop of double cream. Taste for seasonings. The sauce should be so good you'll want to eat it all now: resist the temptation, and pour it over the shellfish in their serving dishes. (If you are using shells you may need to cut the scallops into smaller pieces.)The next bit is unorthodox, but makes all the difference to the dish. Grate strong cheddar generously over the top and put under a hot grill to brown just before serving. The crusty melted cheese contrasts with the shellfish and sauce to fine effect. Give your guests teaspoons as well as little forks and you will have no need for mashed potato piped round the edge, which is sometimes just an excuse for an inadequate amount of scallops.

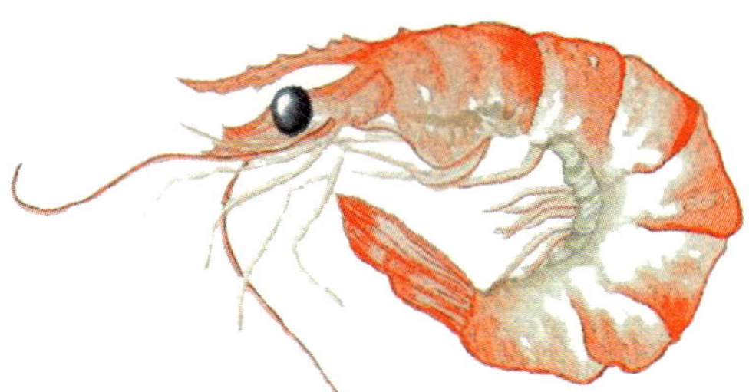

## Green Thai Fish Curry – Alan Megahey

Serves 4

*1 red onion*
*1 red or yellow pepper*
*Coriander leaves*
*1 clove garlic*
*Cumin*
*Lime juice*
*Oil*
*Thai fish sauce*
*Garam marsala, star anise*
*275ml (½ pint) coconut milk or single cream*
*1 or 2 glasses white wine*
*Lemon grass*
*900g (2 lb) fish pieces*
*Juice of half a lemon*
*Oyster and soy sauce*
*Salt*
*Handful of capers*
*Spring onion, coriander, parsley, thyme, freshly chopped*

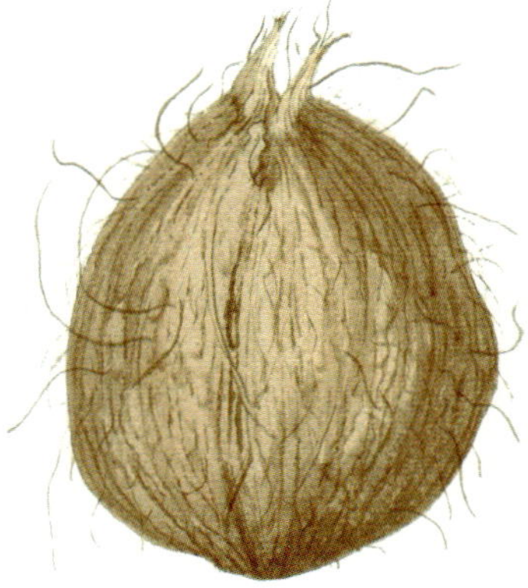

Sauté some red onion (or ordinary onion if you haven't red) and maybe a yellow pepper (or red) in olive oil, until tender. To this, add a mixture of coriander leaves, a garlic clove, a sprinkling of cumin, some lime juice and some oil (Thai fish sauce if you have it) which you have made into a paste in the liquidizer. If you don't want to be bothered with this paste, then simply sprinkle the cooking onion with ground coriander and ground cumin (and you can add some garam marsala and star anise if you wish), and cook some more. You can also add some garlic paste and anchovy paste if you have it.

When softened, add about half a pint of fish stock and cook some more; then add half a pint of coconut milk (if you have it: if you haven't, use single cream) and a glass or two of white wine. Cook gently, with - if you have them - Kaffir lime leaves and or lemon grass, and or dried coriander and dried lemon grass.

Take about 2lbs of fish pieces (bits of cod, haddock, salmon are ideal) and zizz them in the microwave for about 2 minutes - so they are almost cooked. Add them, plus any liquor they may have generated, to the mixture above and cook slowly. Toss in about half a lemon's worth of juice, a dash of lime juice (if you have it) and a slosh of oyster sauce and soy sauce. A sprinkling of salt will help. Bring the liquid to the boil briefly, and add a good handful of capers. Take off the heat, sprinkle with a mixture of fresh chopped coriander, parsley, thyme and lots of chopped spring onion. Bring to table and serve with rice, or with couscous.

NOTA BENE:

* It will work with only a selection of the herbs/spices/condiments mentioned above. Do not worry. You can experiment!
* You can get concentrated lime juice in small bottles which I find is wonderful - don't use it too liberally!
* You can get garlic and anchovy in tubes of paste - very useful for above.

## Mediterranean Shellfish – Derek Bourgeois

Quick and easy to prepare, this dish can be made equally successfully using most shellfish as the fish base either separately or mixed. Prawns or scallops are the most obvious contenders, but mussels, crab, langoustines or lobster would be suitable. As a starter, it will remind your fish-loving friends of Mediterranean holidays. Serves six.

*75ml (3 fl oz) of good quality olive oil*
*1 medium Spanish onion, finely chopped*
*1 clove garlic, crushed*
*6 button mushrooms, diced*
*6 cherry tomatoes, quartered*
*1 medium – large courgette, thinly sliced then quartered*
*1 tablespoon of tomato puree*
*2 tablespoons of pouring cream*
*1 small glass of Madeira, or dry sherry*
*8 basil leaves, finely chopped (or equivalent dried basil)*
*450g (1 lb) peeled prawns or 32 medium scallops*

Heat the olive oil in a large frying pan. Add the garlic and onion and fry until it starts to brown. Add the mushrooms, tomatoes and courgette and fry gently until golden, stirring regularly. Stir in the tomato puree, basil and wine and cook for a minute or two. Add the shellfish and continue to stir for another two minutes. Finally stir in the cream, heat through and serve immediately.

## Monkfish Aloynius – Derek Bourgeois

When shopping to make this colourful and easy dish, ensure that you really do have the tails and not the centre of the fish, which is much less tender. Serves four.

*900g (2 lbs) monkfish tails*
*1 red pepper, sliced*
*1 green pepper, sliced*
*1 orange/yellow pepper, sliced*
*1 Spanish onion, finely chopped*
*225g (½ lb) squash – Patti pan halved (or sliced courgette)*
*Handful of dried methi (fenugreek) leaves, or cumin*
*Squeeze of tomato puree*
*Milk*
*Juice of 1 lemon*
*225g (½ lb) butter*
*Olive oil*

Poach the monkfish in milk until the flesh is easily separated from the bone. Reserve the flesh and juices.

Fry the onion with the squash (courgette) and peppers in the olive oil until cooked. Add the juices from the poached monkfish. Flake the fish and add to the mixture. Add a generous squeeze of tomato puree, the lemon juice, the butter, and the handful of methi leaves. Warm thoroughly and serve.

## Plaice with Asparagus Sauce – Tidal Favourites

Fillets of plaice are delicious simply grilled. The best fish we have ever eaten was a huge plaice, speared just off Durdle Door only forty minutes before we ate it. Trish Rudd, who brought it to us, kindly cleaned it, and put it under the grill with sea salt, black pepper, lemon juice, butter and fresh rosemary. It needed to be accompanied only by buttered new potatoes and broccoli. That one fish fed four of us to repletion. However, we don't have access to fish so excellent all the time. Sometimes plaice fillets need a bit of help with "goo" if you don't like your meals too dry. The delicacy of the asparagus doesn't overwhelm the flavour of the fish, and the astringency of the lemon juice and yogurt offsets the smoothness of the butter and Boursin. The quantities are up to you; do you like a little to savour or a lot to slosh?

*1 fillet of plaice per person*

Season these with:

*Sea salt, black pepper*
*Small dashes of Tabasco or other piquant pepper or balsamic sauce*
*Fresh or dried herbs, such as rosemary or tarragon*
*Olive oil or butter, dotted*

These will take only about ten minutes to grill, so get the potatoes on first! Then make the sauce: (quantities given for six, but you can vary them)

*Asparagus (allow about five spears per person)*
*135g (½ a pack) butter*
*75g (½ a pack) Boursin garlic and herb cheese*
*Juice of 1 lemon*
*Sea salt, black pepper, several dashes of Tabasco*
*2 teaspoons sugar*
*250ml (½ a tub) Greek yogurt*

Blanche the asparagus in boiling salted water until just tender. Don't chuck the water yet! Meanwhile, put all the rest of the ingredients into the blender or processor. Add the cooked asparagus and half of its water. Chobble until smooth. Heat through and taste for seasoning just before serving, adding more of the boiling water if the sauce is too thick.

## Purbeck Plaice – Xenia Johnston

A tasty supper dish – popular with everyone I've tried it on.

Serves four.

*8 canned sardines*
*8 level tablespoons fresh white breadcrumbs*
*2 level tablespoons finely chopped parsley*
*1 lemon, juice and finely grated peel*
*1 level teaspoon finely grated onion*
*1 level teaspoon salt*
*Beaten egg to bind*
*8 small skinned plaice fillets (about 75g or 3oz each)*
*Knob melted butter*

Mash sardines finely. Combine with crumbs, parsley, lemon peel, onion and salt. Bind loosely with egg. Spread the sardine mixture over plaice fillets and roll up. Arrange them in a buttered shallow heatproof dish. Coat with lemon juice combined with melted butter. Cover dish with lid of foil. Bake in a moderate oven 180C (350F or gas mark 4) for thirty minutes.

## Sally Lee's Tips

**Sole and Plaice:** To skin easily – leave in ice-cold water for a short time.

## Savoury Tuna and Pasta Bake – Linda Brewer

Serves four.

*2 x 185g tins Tuna Flakes*
*1 x 326g tin Sweet Corn*
*250g Pasta Shapes*
*570ml (1 pint) cheese sauce*
*Grated cheese for topping*

Cook pasta shapes in boiling water until soft. Mix together tuna and sweet corn in ovenproof dish, and then add the pasta. Pour over the cheese sauce, making sure all the ingredients are covered. Sprinkle over the grated cheese and place in a hot oven, 180 C (350F) for thirty minutes until brown. Serve with warm Focaccia bread and green salad.

## Seared Tuna with Mashed Sweet Potato – Gareth Jones

The combination of meaty fish, beefy stock and sweet potato in this dish is surprisingly good. Quantities are **per person.**

*1 fresh tuna steak*
*1 sweet potato*
*Knob of unsalted butter*
*Salt and pepper*
*Veal or beef stock, or consommé*
*Parsley*

Season the tuna and sear under high heat, or fry in a hot pan in a little oil. Deglaze the pan with the beef stock, which can be your own, from a cube, or tinned consommé. Serve with boiled sweet potato, mashed with black pepper and unsalted butter. Decorate with parsley.

## All-purpose American Shellfish Chowder – Geoffrey Donald

The basis of this recipe is the traditional New England clam chowder from the north-east coast of the United States. The large native clams were boiled with potatoes to make a healthy and filling soup for the farm workers. In fact any tasty shellfish can be tried, prawns, mussels, even crabmeat, but a favourite is the mixed 'seafood salad' to be found in most delicatessens.
For about four helpings:

*A knob of butter*
*One large onion, skinned and small-sliced*
*3 medium potatoes, peeled and diced sugar-cube size*
*About 300ml (½ pint) boiling water (more may be added)*
*225g (8oz) shellfish seafood (own choice) washed in a colander*
*570ml (1 pint) fresh milk*
*50g (2oz) cheese (cheddar?), grated*
*Salt and pepper (remember seafood itself can be salty)*
*Chopped parsley for garnish*

Melt the butter in a large pan and sauté the onion until golden but not browning. Add the boiling water, potatoes and seasoning and simmer for 20 minutes or so until the potatoes are soft and nearly crumbling. It may be necessary to add a little more water to cover the potatoes while cooking. If appropriate, now is the time to put the pan to one side for reheating later, as the shellfish should be added near to serving time. When ready, pour in the milk, add the seafood and bring back to a simmer. Do not boil for any length of time, as this tends to turn shellfish leathery. Finally, stir in the cheese and serve with a sprinkling of parsley.

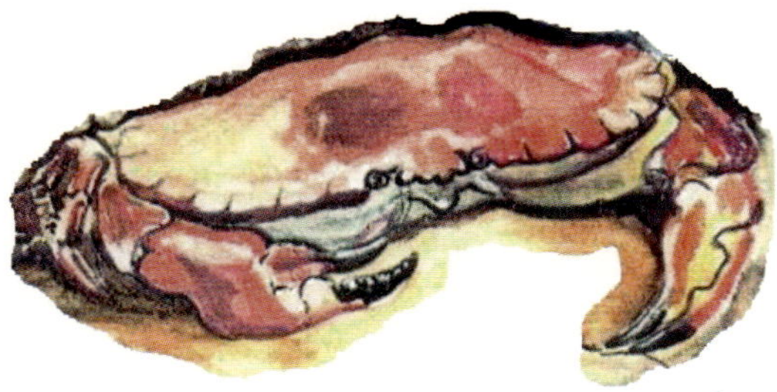

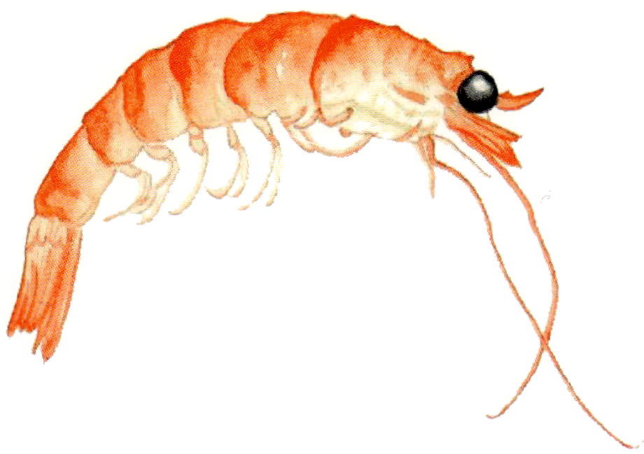

## Simple Salmon with Sophisticated Sauce – Tidal Favourites

Quickly prepared salmon steaks can be transformed into dinner party fare by this sauce, but beware! It is very rich, and you only need a couple of spoons per person, unless your guests like it as much as ours seem to…

For the salmon:

*1 salmon fillet per person*
*Olive oil*
*Lime juice*
*Caster sugar*
*Grainy French mustard*
*Sea salt and black pepper*

Lay the salmon fillets onto a little olive oil in an ovenproof dish. Sprinkle lime juice all over them. (One juicy lime will do about six fillets.) Shake the merest suspicion of caster sugar onto them (about a teaspoon for six.) Salt, pepper and lightly coat them with mild mustard. Cover with foil and bake at about 200C (400F) for twenty-five minutes. You can vary the temperature and timing to suit your timetable.

Meanwhile, make the sauce:

*½ an onion, very finely chopped*
*Knob of butter*
*2 dessertspoons dried horseradish or fresh if you have it*
*2 dessertspoons grainy mustard*
*1 teaspoon sugar*
*Juice of 1 lime*
*1 500ml tub crème fraîche*
*1 150g-pack Boursin garlic and fines herbes cheese*
*A good handful of parsley and thyme, snipped fine*
*Tabasco sauce and cayenne pepper to taste*
*Sea salt and pepper*

Soften the finely chopped onion in the butter and then add the other ingredients in the order given, stirring all the while. If, when all is melted together, it really is too thick to be remotely moral, thin it with a little milk. Taste for seasoning: it should have plenty of bite, but needn't take the roof off your mouth… Serve in a sauceboat, but keep a little back in case it runs out before it gets to the cook!

## Simple Scallops – Liz Rudd

This easy recipe is ideal for when, perhaps on holiday by the sea, you have access to succulent, sweet fresh scallops. However, thawed frozen ones also work well. Good enough for dinner parties, easy enough for family.

For a starter, you will need, per person:

*3 or 4 scallops, with corals if possible*

For a main course, you must know the appetites of your diners: allow at least six per head.

Put the washed scallops into a bowl. Cover them with:

*Equal parts grape-seed (or olive oil) and Oloroso sherry (or Madeira)*
*Plenty of fresh parsley, snipped finely*
*Garlic, more or less, as you like it, squeezed or finely chopped*
*Black pepper and a smidgen of sea salt*

Stir and leave in the fridge to marinate for 2 or 3 hours, covered. Turn them occasionally until you are ready to cook them. Just before you want to serve them, slip the shellfish with their marinade into a heated wok-type pan and keep turning them over high-ish heat until they change colour. This will not take long at all, as they toughen if overcooked. About 2 or 3 minutes is usually enough, except for vast quantities. Serve on their own for a starter, or over rice, with a salad on the side for a main course.

## Tasty Tuna Supper – Sally Pinnock

When there are hungry mouths to feed at the end of a long day on the beach (or at work!) this makes a quick and popular supper dish. It feeds four to six.

*1 large clove garlic*
*1 tablespoon olive oil*
*2 rounded tablespoons tomato purée*
*1 tin tuna in brine*
*300ml (10 fl oz) single cream (Elmlea if wished)*
*75g (2½ oz) pasta*
*1 tablespoon fresh basil, chopped, (or a good pinch dried)*
*Seasoning*

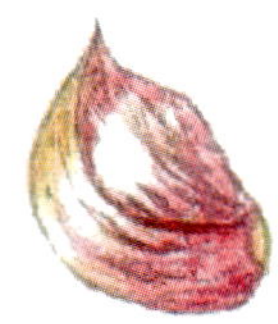

Put the oil into a small pan and add the crushed garlic. Cook over gentle heat until soft. Drain the tuna and add to the pan with the tomato purée, basil and seasoning, stirring all the time. Pour in the cream and mix gently but thoroughly. The sauce should be a lovely salmon pink colour; if it's too pale add more purée. Put the sauce to the side.

Boil a large pan of salted water and add the pasta and cook according to the directions on the package. Drain and put in a serving dish; pour the sauce over the pasta and serve immediately with grated Parmesan cheese and a green salad.

## Sole Portofino – Kevin Booker

This is a dish from the Grill Room of the Hyde Park Hotel where I was Fish Chef back in the seventies.

In this recipe the fish is poached whole, but if you prefer, fillets of sole will work equally well. Serves four.

*4 x 450g (1lb) Dover or lemon sole*
*125g (4½ oz) butter*
*50g (2oz) plain flour*
*28g (1oz) chopped shallots*
*125g (4½ oz) Dolcelatte cheese*
*125ml (4 fl oz) dry Vermouth*
*300ml (½ pint) fish stock*
*300ml (½ pint) double cream*
*Salt and pepper*

Remove skin and head: trim fins and tail. (Keep all trimmings and bones to make fish stock.)

Butter a tin large enough to take your fish and sprinkle shallots over the base. Add the fish and season with salt and milled pepper. Pour over the fish stock and Vermouth and cover with buttered greaseproof paper. Cook in a fairly hot pre-heated oven. Fish on the bone will take fifteen to twenty minutes to cook, whereas filleted fish will cook in eight to ten minutes.

Drain the cooking liquid into a saucepan and keep the fish warm. Bring the liquid to the boil and boil until it has reduced by half. Melt 50g of butter and mix with the flour. Whisk this into the boiling liquid until it thickens. Reduce the heat and mix in the Dolcelatte cheese and the double cream. Bring the sauce back to the boil and remove immediately from the heat. Dress your fish onto warm plates and coat with the sauce.

Note: this dish is fairly rich so I would serve only plain vegetables or a salad with perhaps some new potatoes.

## Stuffed Squid with Raisins and Pine Nuts – Derek Bourgeois

Mediterranean fishy dishes are good news. This one looks as if it has taken many hours to prepare, although it is actually very quick to make, especially if you have a microwave. It also looks spectacular, and does equally well as a starter for dinner, or a lunch dish served with a salad. Serves four to six as a starter or four as a lunch dish.

*1 medium sized squid, the body of which is about 13 – 15 cm (6 – 8 inches) long*
*Good quality olive oil to cover the bottom of a medium sized frying pan*
*1 small onion, finely chopped*
*2 cloves of garlic, very thinly sliced*
*1 medium sized pepper (any colour), diced*
*2 tablespoons of tomato puree*
*50g (2oz) pine nuts*
*75g (3oz) raisins*
*1 small glass of dry white wine*

If the squid is whole cut off the head and wings and remove all the innards. It is important to ensure that the squid will not leak when stuffed.
Heat the olive oil in the bottom of a medium sized frying pan. Fry the onions, garlic, raisins, pine nuts and pepper until soft. Add the tomato puree and white wine, and stir until a thick, creamy texture is achieved that is not too liquid. Stuff the squid with this mixture.

Bake in the oven for forty to forty-five minutes at 140C (275F) placing in such a way that the stuffing will be retained. Alternatively put into a microwave and cook on a high setting for 3 minutes. To serve, slice the squid carefully into rings making sure that the stuffing remains inside the rings.

## Yvonne Adams' Fish Recipes

A lot of people avoid fish because they hate the smell or don't like the messy washing-up. But, in these days of the microwave, cooking fish couldn't be easier. Usually it's best to get it filleted, or cut into cutlets. Then, unless you want sushi, it's just six minutes in a covered, vented dish with the appropriate seasonings and that's it.

Unless it's for a pie or to use up leftovers (which are probably best mixed with rice or pasta) any fish that's absolutely drowned in sauce suggests that the cook is trying to disguise that something is wrong. For presentation, just a dollop of something special (even out of a bottle), and a sprig of herbs like fennel or alexanders, that grow wild in this area, is all you need.

The answer to all my prayers for both fresh and seawater fish is Culpepper's Fish seasoning, in little blue drums. I've matched all the ingredients but nothing I do is quite so good. I even take it abroad with me. (Concerning bought products, I remember Fanny Craddock saying nothing could beat a packet of Bread Sauce).

Any kind of flat fish needs to be kept a day in the fridge. Skate needs to be kept even longer, either in a bucket of saltwater, in the fridge, or even in the freezer for three days. Fishermen used to peg them out on the washing line. The skin exudes a thick gelatinous mucus, which can smell of ammonia sometimes, if you attempt to eat it too fresh. This needs to be washed off. Other newly-caught flat fish, like plaice, turbot, brill, etc. need keeping to plump the flesh up, otherwise the moisture evaporates too quickly and the fish goes into disastrous holes!

Whole fish like salmon, trout, mackerel and so on must be eaten as fresh as possible. Scour (slice) two or three times each side to allow the heat in and to stop the fish exploding in the microwave.

Shredded seaweed, cabbage or spinach mixed with a little sugar and fried is a good accompaniment to most fish dishes. Sliced black olives with very white fish like bream, bass or mullet is good.

If you are not making your own sauce, a pot of Hollandaise, Tartar or Dill Sauce is always a good standby, kept in the fridge. Just a spoonful on the plate is all you need, with a sprig of fennel or a few slivers of red, orange, yellow or green peppers. As in France or Spain, an Aioli or Rouille (red chilli) sauce are good too, especially on toast or croutons, with a fish soup.

Sometimes I bake pastry in real scallop shells, and these make a pretty display.

I used to dread having to cook conger or dogfish, but now I poach it and let it cool. Then, if the skin hasn't been removed, it's easier to scrape it off. Either fish, arranged on a long plate on a bed of chicory and asparagus, with a mayonnaise sauce and chopped capers and/or gherkins, can be prepared in advance for a party and served cold. Alternatively, serve with a tomato-based sauce, either hot or cold.

## Tomato Sauce

*1 onion or shallot, chopped*
*5 crushed cloves garlic*
*4 tablespoons olive oil*
*700g (1½ lbs) ripe tomatoes, chopped (or tinned)*
*1 tablespoon sugar*
*2 tablespoons raspberry vinegar*
*1 tablespoon chopped parsley*
*1 tablespoon chopped basil*
*Salt and pepper*
*1 cup water*

Sauté the onions and garlic in the oil until golden. Add all the rest of the ingredients and simmer gently for half an hour. Liquidise and serve hot or cold.

## Mayonnaise Sauce

*1 tablespoon mayonnaise + chopped parsley, tarragon and basil*

Or:

*1 tablespoon mayonnaise + chopped capers and gherkins*

Mix either base with

*1 teaspoon mustard*
*3 chopped anchovy fillets*

## Scollops – Scallops

*4 per person*
*1 shallot, finely chopped*
*25g (1oz) butter*
*150ml (¼ pint) double cream*
*Small glass white wine*
*Salt and pepper*
*Chopped parsley*

Local scollops are so big and juicy it would be piggish to eat more than four… To prepare them, open with an oyster knife, remove frilly skirt and black bile duct, leaving the plump meaty muscle and orange roe. Fry chopped shallot (or small onion) in butter until transparent and add all the other ingredients except the scollops. Mix well. Turn off heat. Place scollops carefully on sauce and cover with close fitting pan lid. Allow scollops to cook lightly in the steam of the sauce. Don't overcook or they shrink and toughen. Serve with a sprinkling of parsley.

## Stuffed Squid

A Maltese fisherman recommended this method to us in 1974.

To clean squid: pull off tentacles and head, nip out beak and ink sac, wash inside body and pull out transparent backbone blade.

Hard-boil eggs, chop and mix with chopped onions and seasoning.

Stuff squid body with this mixture and seal with head and tentacles. If it is large, bake it in the oven with a little oil to stop it sticking to the pan. If small, fry in pan on top of stove. The squid go dark pink when cooked.

## Taramasalata or Tarama

Taramasalata is Greek fish roe paté, and tarama is Greek dried grey mullet roe. Quantities and proportions are variable: Greek islanders rarely use cookery books – they make it how their mothers taught them, and that varies widely…

*200g (7oz) smoked cod's roe, or tarama, or fresh cod's roe and salt*
*6 slices crustless white bread, soaked in water and squeezed*
*Juice of 1 or 2 lemons*
*150ml (¼ pint) olive oil and/or 6 tablespoons double cream*
*Pepper*

Scoop the roe out of the skin (after cooking if fresh hard cod's roe is being used). Then either pound the ingredients in a mortar or use a blender. Gradually add lemon juice, pepper, olive oil/cream, until you have a thick paste. (If impatient, add 1 level teaspoon gelatine dissolved in 3 teaspoons water.) Put in the fridge to solidify.

For variation you can add ¼ of a Spanish onion, grated, and/or 1-2 cloves of garlic, chopped very fine.

Sprinkle with chopped parsley and garnish with black olives. Serve with hot toast or crudités such as carrot, celery and cucumber. If you like that supermarket pinkness you can add a little beetroot juice.

To impress unexpected dinner guests with impromptu starters, all the above can be made from a well-stocked larder. Tinned roes, cream, bottled lemon juice, pickled beetroot juice, box of Melba toast or dip fingers; all can be pressed into service.

## Grandmother's Remedies – Sally Lee

Light suppers make long days.

## Brill under the Grill – Tidal Favourites

Fresh brill is a wonderful treat, and, treated simply, hard to beat…

*1 fillet per person (2 if they are small)*
*Olive oil*
*Lime or lemon juice*
*Dash of Tabasco*
*Sea salt and black pepper*

You can mix the oil and seasonings in a little jug to pour over the fish, or simply drizzle them one at a time. Also, you can do this earlier in the day and leave them to marinate in the fridge, or do your drizzling just before you pop them under a hot grill for five minutes. Test with a knife to see if the flesh is milky white but still firm: if it is still transparent in the middle, it needs another minute or two. We love it served with broccoli and Hollandaise sauce.

Brill can also be cooked in good olive oil in a wok or frying pan: add a squeeze more lime or lemon juice and a little grainy mustard to the juices in the pan after taking out the cooked fish, and it makes its own delicious sauce.

# Main Courses

**Jersey Calf, Rectory Farm, Winfrith Newburgh**
The farm is organically managed.

This is the section that vegetarians will eschew, as most main courses consist of meat. However, there is, today, a strong movement away from the cruelty of factory farming, back to the humane methods of animal husbandry practised by our forebears. More shoppers are demanding that their meat be naturally reared and despatched with the least possible stress to the animals. (Natural death can, of course, occasion much suffering from disease and age.) We cannot, in all conscience, eat beasts that have not led normal, happy, farm-animal lives. We are lucky, here in Dorset, to see our cows contentedly chewing in the meadows, pigs snuffling under trees and lambs springing on our hills. There are fine farms rearing birds of all sorts in the open air, protected from predators. They can all grow under ideal conditions on good Dorset grass in good Dorset air: our countryside would be infinitely poorer without them. We also have some superb butchers, such as the Curtis shops in Wareham and Mr Blake the Butcher in Wool, who know the provenance of their meat and aim to supply from local sources. Like our churches, they deserve our support, or we shall deserve to lose them.

## Beef

**Jersey Mama, Rectory Farm, Winfrith Newburgh**

Jersey cows are bred for their rich creamy milk, of course. This one was so beautiful that I could not resist including her at the head of the beef section.

## Veal with Turmeric and Cream – Tidal Favourites

For many years I refused to use veal, as I could not bear to think of the calves leading a horrible, crated life. Happily, veal now grown in England is naturally reared on the mother cow, and is a healthy rose pink colour. That, at least, is how I buy it, from John Blake, in Wool. This recipe works equally well, however, with fillet of pork chunks, or lamb. You can also use the same ingredients to stir-fry the remains of the Sunday roast.

For **each person** you need:

*110g (¼ lb) cubed veal, or meat of choice*
*¼ onion, chopped*
*Mushrooms, as many as you like, chopped*
*1 clove garlic, chopped*
*A teaspoon or so of peeled ginger, finely chopped, if liked*
*1 teaspoon turmeric, or more, to taste*
*Sea salt and black pepper, Tabasco or chilli powder, to taste (optional)*
*Olive oil for frying*
*Splash of sherry*
*Cream, or crème fraîche, or Boursin garlic and fines herbes cheese, a little or a lot, as liked*

Soften the onion in the oil; then the mushrooms and garlic. Add the meat, sprinkle with the spices and seasonings and stir-fry until just cooked through. Splash in the sherry or other suitable booze, and add the cream or creams of your choice. Check seasonings and serve immediately, perhaps over rice, or with new potatoes and a green vegetable or two.

My husband likes the flavour and wonderful fragrance of the turmeric, but I leave out the hotter things until he has had his helping. Then I wickedly add chilli and Tabasco until it sparkles, without blowing one's mouth apart…

## Beef Stew with Black Olives – Geoffrey Donald

This is a wholesome beef stew fortified with red wine and with the olives in addition to more traditional vegetables. It therefore contains some unusual flavours.

For about six servings:

*900g (2lb) of best stewing steak*
*3 or 4 rashers of bacon, lean or streaky as desired*
*A knob of butter and olive oil for frying*
*275ml (½ pint) stock, beef or chicken*
*275ml (½ pint) red wine*
*A medium onion, chopped small*
*2 cloves garlic, crushed or chopped finely*
*2 level tablespoons cornflour*
*A sprinkling of thyme, fresh or dried*
*Salt to taste (say a level teaspoon or two)*
*A dozen small onions, skinned*
*225g (8oz) small button mushrooms, washed*
*225g (8oz) peas, fresh or frozen*
*2 or three carrots, cleaned and medium sliced*
*110g (4oz) black olives (large Greek ones)*

Cut the bacon into inch squares and fry until crisp in a little of the oil. Put aside into a large flameproof casserole, such as Le Creuset. Cut the steak into one-inch cubes, discarding any undesirable parts, and fry these a few at a time in the oil and butter until well browned. Red meat often exudes water when heated and tends to boil in the frying pan rather than searing at a higher temperature. Pour off any excess liquid into a cup for use later. Only when the steamy bubbling turns into a healthy sizzle is the meat browning effectively. Add the meat to the casserole together with any leftover juices. Reserve a third of the stock for later and add the rest to the casserole. Add the wine, chopped onion, garlic, thyme and salt. Bring to the boil, reduce the heat and simmer gently with the lid on for a couple of hours. If it is now allowed to cool and stand overnight, the flavours will develop further.

On serving day, cook the small onions and sliced carrots in boiling salted water for ten minutes or so. Add the mushrooms and peas and simmer for a further five minutes.

Reheat the casserole if necessary. Blend the flour into the last of the stock and pour in, stirring the while, to thicken the juices. Strain the vegetables and add with the olives. Mix thoroughly and simmer for a further few minutes before serving.

## Celebration Beef – Tidal Favourites

There are times in life when just the two of you want to celebrate: it may be a quiet anniversary, the end of the mortgage, having a rare evening without the children or guests in the house, a minor birthday or a small lottery win. You want to eat something special, but not to spend all day slaving over it; nor do you want to expend much energy on clearing up, as you might have better things to do with the rest of your evening… If you can buy splendid locally grown beef, as luckily we can in Dorset, you might like to try this simple way of cooking it next time you are quietly celebrating.

*4 or 5 slices of fillet steak each, cut very thin*
*A generous glass of sherry or Madeira*
*Plentiful shakes of Soy sauce, Worcester Sauce, Tabasco*
*Several good turns of the pepper mill*
*1 clove chopped garlic (more if you're garlic freaks)*
*Olive oil and butter*

Have your butcher slice the beef very thinly. (John Blake in Wool will do it beautifully for you.) Perhaps the best way to judge how many slices you will need is to decide how thick you would like a normal steak to be and ask him to slice that much into wafers. Marinate your slices in the sherry, sauces, pepper and garlic for as much or as little time as you have.

Have your favourite potatoes ready (we like them sliced and layered in a dish with fried onions, salt, pepper and grated cheese on top, baked for an hour or so: plain-boiled new potatoes in season are good too). Also have your green vegetables almost cooked (our favourites are asparagus or mange-tout peas), or prepare a side salad. When you are only two minutes from eating heat the oil and a dollop of butter in a frying pan. (I like a wok-type pan best). Slide in your slices of beef with their marinade, making sure that each slice lies flat. Turn immediately and after a few seconds remove from the pan onto hot plates. Add some more grinds of the pepper mill to the juices in the pan and pour as a sauce over the beef.

Serve with the vegetables and persuade the butler to produce his finest wine. Candles and flowers might come into it somewhere. Your evening should take off from there.

## Convalescent's Casserole – Tidal Favourites

When you have friends nearby where the chief cook is temporarily out of commission, this is a good, nourishing all in one dish. Take it along with some ready to cook mange-tout peas or broccoli, with another comfort food such as Baked Egg Custard or Lemon Mousse for pudding, and recovery will be imminent.

For **each person** you need:

*110g (¼ lb) cubed good lean beef steak, with some kidney if liked*
*½ chopped onion*
*1 chopped carrot*
*Handful of chopped mushrooms*
*½ chopped red pepper*
*1 medium-sized washed potato with the skin on*
*Olive oil for frying and drizzling*
*Flour or cornflour, seasoned with sea salt, black pepper, and 1 teaspoon of cocoa per person*
*Red wine to cover meat*
*Rosemary, bay leaves, Worcester sauce*

Soften the vegetables in a little oil over medium heat, in a flameproof casserole. Meanwhile shake the meat in a plaggy bag with the flour, cocoa and dry seasonings. Add to the casserole and keep turning while it changes colour. It will burn easily if you don't keep it on the move. Cover with red wine and add the herbs and Worcester sauce. Bring to simmer. Remove from heat and layer on thickly sliced potatoes; season with salt and plenty of black pepper and drizzle olive oil or melted butter over them. Cook in a low oven (about 150C, 300F) for up to two hours, or at a higher temperature for an hour or so. If it smells good, it's done. It is perfectly possible to enjoy this without the excuse of being ill…

## Dorset Oxtail Stew – Tidal Favourites

It is a mystery why we still call this "oxtail", when we no longer grow oxen in this country. The French probably call it "queue de boeuf", which is more sensible. It has a unique, succulent texture and flavour, and few things are more comforting, on a raw autumn or winter day, than coming home to the smell of oxtail stew wafting from the oven. If you put lightly oiled and salted un-peeled potatoes beside it for the last two hours or so of cooking, and serve with lots of crinkly Savoy cabbage, you will have the most nourishing and warming meal imaginable.

Quantities are variable according to how much meat you have. This is a rough guide:

*1 large and 1 small tail section per person. (This usually works out at 2 tails for 8-10 people.)*
*3 or 4 chopped onions*
*3 or more chopped garlic cloves (more is better)*
*Sliced carrots, a large one per person*
*Several bayleaves*
*Olive oil for frying*
*At least a bottle, or half of a wine-box of robust red wine*

Gently fry the vegetables in a large flameproof casserole, until softened. Shake the oxtail sections in a plastic bag with:

*Flour or cornflour (you will need at least 2 tablespoons)*
*Sea salt, (at least 2 dessertspoons), plenty of black pepper*
*Cocoa (at least 2 dessertspoons)*

Put the seasoned meat into the softened vegetables with the bayleaves in the casserole and keep turning over medium heat until the pieces change colour. Then cover with lots of red wine, or wine and water. Bring to the boil and put in a low-ish oven to simmer for about 3 hours. It is even better if you can let it stand overnight so that you can skim off the fat when cold and reheat it next evening. Check for seasonings; this dish needs more salt than you would think. If it tastes flat and boring, you didn't use enough salt at the flour-in-plaggy-bag stage, but you can rescue it with more now. It should be a wonderful, redolent mass, with the meat falling easily off the bone.

## Kevin Booker, Head Chef at Cranleigh School

# Cranleigh Cooks . . .

My husband Andrew taught at Cranleigh School, in Surrey, for twenty-eight years. The design above was used for the cover of a cookbook we produced in the seventies to help raise money for a new boarding house. Plus ça change! The school is fortunate to have Kevin Booker as Chef. A professional to his fingertips, he not only feeds large numbers of hungry people every day, but rises magnificently to "state" occasions. He is highly valued by all, not only for his superb cooking, but also for his friendship; it is from this privileged position that we were able to persuade him to give us some of his recipes. In addition to Sirloin Booker, there is more of his expertise in the Fish, Lunch Dishes, Barbecue and Savoury Sauce sections.

## Sirloin Booker

A regular on our function menus at the school: this version serves six. You will need to allow *225-280g (8-10oz) of sirloin per person.* Ask your butcher to cut you a middle piece from the sirloin. Trim away all the fat and sinew with a sharp knife. (Keep the trimmings for the sauce.) Cut the sirloin in half across the grain of the meat, as in fig. 1. Tie each piece of meat with three or four strings, as in fig 2. Cover meat with marinade and refrigerate overnight.

For the marinade:

fig 1

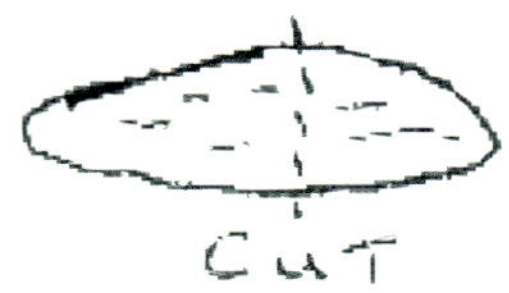


*300ml (3/4 pint) red wine*
*150ml (1/4 pint) Madeira wine*
*1 carrot, peeled and chopped*
*1 onion, peeled and chopped*
*1 stick celery, washed and chopped*
*1 leek, washed and chopped*
*1 bay leaf, 1 sprig of thyme, 12 peppercorns*

fig 2.

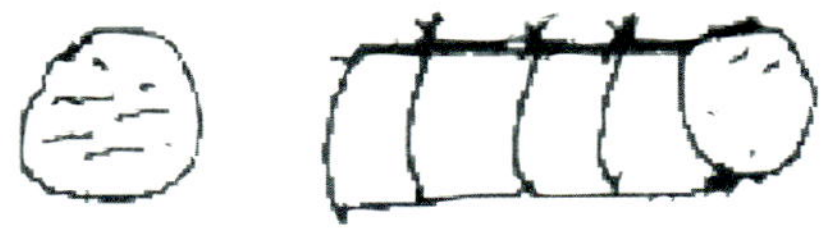

As in all cooking, timing is probably the most important aspect; getting everything ready together is an art all of its own. The sauce for this dish can be made well in advance, leaving you time to do other things: so – remove the meat from the marinade and return the meat to the fridge.

Sirloin Booker, continued

For the sauce:

*125g (4½ oz) butter*
*125g (4½ oz) plain flour*
*1 tablespoon tomato purée*
*600ml (just over 1 pint) beef stock (cube is fine)*
*Sirloin trimmings*
*The marinade*

Heat the butter in a large saucepan and brown the meat trimmings and the vegetables from the marinade. Add the tomato purée and cook for two more minutes. Add the flour and mix in. Slowly add the stock and the liquid from the marinade. Bring to the boil and turn down the heat until the sauce is just simmering. Allow the sauce to cook out for thirty minutes. Check the seasoning and strain into a clean saucepan ready for use.

To cook the sirloin:

Start to cook the sirloin about an hour before you are ready to eat.

Season with salt and milled pepper. Heat a little oil in a frying pan until it starts to smoke. Carefully brown the meat on all sides and place in a roasting tin. Cook in a fairly hot pre-heated oven. The marinade has tenderised the meat, so ten to fifteen minutes is all it will take to keep the sirloin pink. Cook a little longer for well-done meat. Keep the sirloin warm and allow it to rest for ten to fifteen minutes.

Re-heat the sauce and remove any excess grease. Slice the meat thickly and serve on a bread crouton. Coat with the sauce.

## Calves' Liver with Mushrooms and Sherry – Alan Smith

How many times have you been about to finish a bottle of dry sherry when, on opening the door of the refrigerator, you have suddenly come across a plate of calves' liver and a bowl of mushrooms and wondered what to do with them? This handy recipe is for just such an occasion. Alternatively, if the following appeals, you could order the liver and mushrooms in advance from your local liver and mushroom centre; if it doesn't, you could just finish the bottle of sherry, secure in the knowledge that your own liver is about to regenerate.

*675g (1½ lb) calves' liver, thinly sliced*
*225g (½ lb) mushrooms*
*Olive oil*
*Butter*
*Fresh rosemary*
*Dry sherry*

Slice mushrooms and fry in a mixture of two parts butter to one part olive oil over a moderate heat until soft. Add slices of liver and continue to fry for not more than a minute, or until they are still slightly pink. Season with a little fresh rosemary, sea salt and freshly ground black pepper to taste. Add one or two glasses of sherry, stir until heated through and serve immediately.

It is easy to economise by using lambs' or pigs' liver; easy to experiment by using some of the more exotic but preferably non-poisonous varieties of mushroom.

## Pasta al Sugo – Geoffrey Bolt

Many years ago, as a young master at Cranleigh School, I found myself talking to my Sixth Form about food, which seemed to us all at the time to be a not unacceptable alternative to the Chemistry that we were doubtless supposed to be discussing.

One of my pupils subsequently told me that he was hoping to entertain some friends to a supper of spaghetti and asked my advice about the sauce to accompany it. I gave him the recipe below, which I learned from my old friend Marcelle Plutoni in Cap d'Ail just after the war, which calls for two or three cloves of garlic.

Uncertain of the precise meaning of the word 'clove', the boy went to the greengrocer and bought three large bulbs of garlic, and proceeded with the preparation of the dish as described below. The dish was eaten but… I don't really need to tell the story any further.

The quantities given should provide enough sauce for decent helpings for four people.

*2 medium-sized onions, finely chopped*
*Oil and butter for frying*
*225g (8oz) good minced beef*
*2 or 3 cloves garlic*
*1 to 2 pints (570ml to 1.2 litres) stock, milk or water*
*1 dessertspoon each of tarragon and basil*
*Salt and pepper*
*175g (6oz) chopped mushrooms*
*1 glass red wine*

Cook the onions in the oil and butter until they are transparent but not brown. Add the minced beef and the garlic and turn in the oil until just brown. Pour about 570ml (1 pint) of the liquid into the pan with the herbs and seasonings to taste.

Stir well and simmer very slowly for not less than three hours, replacing the liquid as it evaporates. Then add the mushrooms and continue to simmer for another hour. The last addition of liquid, perhaps twenty minutes before serving, should be the glass of red wine.

The pasta should be boiled in salted water to which a tablespoon of olive oil has been added, which in some mysterious way prevents the strands of spaghetti sticking together. When just cooked, as found by frequent tasting, strain and return to the saucepan. Now add a teaspoonful of oil, turn the spaghetti in this and add two-thirds of the sauce.

Mix well and serve, adding the remainder of the sauce to the top of each helping. Parmesan cheese should be available to those who like it.

A glass or three of Chianti goes very well with this dish, which many people find is an interesting change from the more usual Bolognese.

## My Mother Said…

It's more important to eat the meal hot than to wash up the pots – leave them to soak until morning.

## Sailors' Fillet of King Prawn – Chef at Sailor's Return, East Chaldon

An ideal dinner party main course, this luxurious combination of fillet steak and king prawn in a boozy cream sauce is quick and easy to make – expensive but well worth it. Treat yourself! Quantities are given for two persons; fifteen minutes preparation time, ten minutes cooking time.

*225g (8oz) fillet steak*
*8 king prawns, shelled and de-veined*
*¼ medium-sized onion*
*50g (2oz) mushrooms*
*150ml (¼ pint) double cream*
*150ml (¼ pint) beef stock*
*Shot of brandy*
*2 sprigs fresh parsley*
*1 teaspoon French mustard*
*1 teaspoon vegetable oil*

Finely dice the onion; wash and slice the mushrooms. Cut the fillet steak into thin strips. Wash and finely chop parsley.

Heat a non-stick pan or wok with the oil and add the fillet steak. Seal off to a golden brown, quickly, but keeping the steak pink. Remove the strips of meat, add the prawns to the pan and cook until the colour is set. Remove from the pan. Sauté the onions until transparent and soft, making sure not to caramelise them. Add the mushrooms and cook until soft.

Deglaze the pan with the shot of brandy; reduce by half. Add the beef stock and reduce by half again. Add the French mustard and the cream and reduce until all the liquid thickens. Add the meat and prawns; heat through and season to taste. Sprinkle with the parsley. This dish can be served with rice or any seasonal potatoes. Happy cooking!

**Sailor's Return, East Chaldon**

## Tagliatelle Trois Chefs – Jilly Palmer

We lived in Libya and the "Trois Chefs" restaurant had the reputation of being the best of a pretty poor selection. To quote an American friend: "Ten thousand flies can't be wrong!" As we boarded the troop ship for home, Julio, the proprietor, came aboard and gave me the recipe. It is a great stand-by for teenage parties and is basically layers of pasta in cheese sauce and a Bolognaise mixture. It will serve about eight normal appetites or four teens.

*1.2 litres (2 pints) rich cheese sauce*
*1 pack tagliatelle*
*Olive oil*
*2 onions*
*900g (2lbs) minced beef*
*1 large tin tomatoes*
*2 tablespoons concentrated tomato purée*
*Sundried tomatoes (maybe)*
*Red wine*
*Salt and pepper*
*Grated cheese for topping*

Make about two pints of rich cheese sauce with the béchamel method. Boil 1 pack of tagliatelle and when cooked toss in olive oil. Fry two chopped onions in olive oil and add 2 lbs minced beef (Julio probably used goat!) Add one large tin of tomatoes, a good two tablespoons of tomato purée and maybe some sundried tomatoes (not invented in 1975), a slurp of cheap red wine and salt and pepper to taste. Put a layer of the tagliatelle in cheese sauce in a dish, then the Bolognaise mixture and another layer of tagliatelle in cheese sauce. Top with lots of grated cheese.

## Sally Lee's Tips

**Yorkshire Pudding:** Sprinkle pepper in the bottom of the tin – it will rise evenly.

Cockerel

## Chicken Chartreuse – Sally Lee

I offer this recipe in fond memory of my friend Margaret. It is excellent for a summer party.

> *3 tablespoons vinegar made up to 550ml (1 pint) with hot water*
> *50g (2oz) Aspic Crystals*
> *225g (½ lb) cooked and cooled peas*

Add the Aspic Crystals to the vinegar/water mixture and stir until dissolved. Combine half of this mixture with the peas; pour into a large (3-pint) ring mould and chill until set. Combine the following ingredients in the remaining half of the Aspic:

> *8 tablespoons thick mayonnaise*
> *5 tablespoons double cream*
> *2 teaspoons lemon juice*
> *1 teaspoon curry powder*
> *350g (¾ lb) cooked chicken cut into small pieces*
> *225g (½ lb) cooked and diced new potatoes*
> *75g (3oz) celery chopped small*
> *6 spring onions or chives, chopped*

Pour this over the set peas in the mould and chill to set. To serve: stand mould in warm water to loosen and turn out onto a dish. Fill the centre with watercress.

## Chicken with Artichoke Hearts – Geoffrey Donald

You will need at least two or three artichoke hearts per person; use chicken breasts with or without skin as desired. Serves four.

*4 chicken breasts*
*Tinned artichoke hearts, drained*
*Flour*
*A knob of butter and olive oil for frying*
*275ml (½ pint) chicken stock*
*2 tablespoons brandy*
*2 teaspoons lemon juice*
*150ml (5fl oz) soured cream*
*Salt and black pepper*

The easy way to coat the chicken breasts is to put them, one at a time, into a plastic food bag with the seasoned flour and shake vigorously. Melt the butter and oil in a frying pan and brown each piece nicely all over. The skin side can be fried a little longer if desired. Transfer to a casserole.

Add a little more butter to the frying pan and reheat before stirring in another tablespoon or so of flour into the hot oils. Quickly pour in the cold stock, stirring vigorously to amalgamate. Add the brandy, lemon juice, and salt and pepper to taste. Continue heating until the sauce has thickened before slowly adding the soured cream; pour over the chicken breasts. Cover and bake in the oven at 180C (350F) for forty minutes. Finally, add the artichoke hearts on top, covering each with a little sauce, and cook for a further quarter of an hour until ready to serve.

## Sticky Chicken – Sheila Morrice

*4/6 chicken breasts or pieces*
*½ cup mango chutney*
*½ cup mayonnaise*
*1 packet brown onion soup mix*
*1 cup water*

Mix all ingredients and pour over chicken. Bake for forty minutes until tender at 170-180 C (325-350 F).

## My Mother Said…

Despite what I say about working quickly in order to get through it, if there's a rainbow or a sunset – watch it! Work will wait.

## Chicken with Cinnamon – Geoffrey Donald

This recipe is based on 'Friar's Chicken' as described by the late travel writer, H. V. Morton, in his book, 'In Scotland Again': "A Scottish dish of great antiquity and a favourite of James VI and I". The original text describes the preparation of a veal stock, but a good homemade chicken stock serves well. A beef-type stock would be too meaty for this recipe. It necessarily starts with a whole farmyard chicken, which is cleaned, separated into legs, wings and body, and then skinned. One can now buy breasts and drumsticks already packed, but why not just a breast apiece for each guest?
Serves four.

*Four chicken breasts or equivalent, skinned*
*570ml (1 pint) chicken stock*
*Powdered cinnamon*
*Salt and black pepper*
*Bunch of parsley*
*Two or three eggs*

Heat the stock in a large pan, remove any undesirable parts from the chicken pieces, and put them in the stock with salt and pepper to taste. Bring to a simmer and leave to cook. Meanwhile take a good bunch of the parsley, chop it quite fine and add to the pan. One of the main flavours comes from the parsley so don't under-do it; a couple of tablespoons should do. Now add a teaspoon or so of cinnamon. Again, this should be a dominant taste, not just a hint, so add enough so that when you taste it later it is really distinctive. An hour of gentle simmer should cook the chicken and develop the flavours in it. Just before serving, check the seasonings and adjust if necessary. A last sprinkle of cinnamon can be added now if desired. Crack the eggs into a bowl and whisk white and yolk together. Remove the pan from the heat and pour in the eggs, stirring gently. Do not be surprised at the unusual appearance! Serve with your choice of vegetables and, as a last garnish, sprinkle a little more fresh, green chopped parsley on top. (Note: if you think your guests might not like the texture of the curdled eggs in this sauce, add them at the last moment, with the liquid well off the boil.)

## Red (Hot) Chicken – Tidal Favourites

Red it is; hot it need be only as much as you like it. You can marinate the pieces in the sauce and part-cook them before finishing them over the barbecue, serving the sauce as a dip for the meat. Casseroled, it is a useful family dish and freezes well.
Quantities are **per person.**

*1 thigh and 1 leg free-range chicken*
*½ chopped red onion*
*½ clove garlic, chopped*
*½ red pepper,chopped*
*Red chilli, chopped fine, a little, a lot or none at all*
*Oil for frying*
*A drizzle of honey over each piece*
*Salt and pepper*
*Cayenne (hot) or paprika (mild), to taste*
*½ tin chopped tomatoes*
*1 glass red wine*

Soften the chopped onion, garlic and peppers in the oil. Add the chicken pieces and lightly brown them on all sides. Drizzle the honey over them and then shake the seasonings and spices onto them. Turn and stir over low heat for a few moments more and then add the tomatoes and red wine. Bring to simmer and then either put them in a medium oven for forty-five minutes or so or use as suggested for a barbecue.

## Squashy Chicken – Hilli Waller

This makes a good autumnal, all-in-one, healthy family meal. Serves four to six.

*1 medium (free range) chicken*
*2 medium onions*
*6 – 10 potatoes, skins on or off depending on type (reds are good)*
*½ small pumpkin*
*1 small butternut squash*
*Olive oil and butter for coating*
*Salt and pepper*
*Small splash red wine*
*Parsley for decoration*

Coat chicken with mixture of olive oil, butter, salt and pepper. Place in hot oven at 220C (425F, gas mark 6/7 top Aga oven) for twenty minutes, basting halfway through this time.

Prepare vegetables by cutting onions into quarters, pumpkin and squash into 1-inch chunks and potatoes into halves or quarters depending on size.

Add the vegetables to the chicken after the first twenty minutes, with salt, pepper and a splash of red wine. Cook for another one to one-and-a-quarter hours, depending on the size of the chicken and vegetables. Stir the vegetables every so often.

Serve the chicken with its vegetables on a large meat platter and decorate with some parsley.

## Swedish Chicken – Ann Brown

Serves four.

*4 chicken joints*
*1½ gills (approximately 200ml, 8 fl oz) chicken stock (cube or home-made)*
*3 tablespoons soy sauce*
*3 tablespoons oil*
*1 dessertspoon brown sugar*
*1 teaspoon dried ginger*
*½ teaspoon dried oregano*
*Salt and pepper*

Take any skin off the chicken joints. Place in an ovenproof dish and season with salt and pepper. Mix the other ingredients and pour over the chicken. Bake in a moderately hot oven for about forty minutes. Serve with rice and vegetables or a salad.

## Tuscan Chicken – Alan Smith

For some reason, I can't remember from whose wine catalogue I pinched this; if I could, I would happily acknowledge it…

*1 chicken piece per person, skin on*
*2 or 3 whole cloves of garlic per person, skin on*
*Fresh rosemary sprigs*
*Sea salt and black pepper*
*Olive oil*

Place chicken pieces, skin up, in a shallow baking tray. Drizzle with olive oil; grind the sea salt and pepper over them; scatter the sprigs of rosemary and garlic cloves round and about them; bake at 180C (350F) for about three-quarters of an hour, or until the skin is crisp.

# Duck

## Duck with Plum Sauce – Yvonne Adams

Wild duck is best for this dish, but farmyard is fine. It makes a change from Duck à l'Orange, and is good if you cannot eat citrus fruit or tomatoes, which can exacerbate arthritis.

*Duck*
*Pot of stir-fry plum sauce*

Marinate the duck in the sauce overnight. Put a lid or foil on it and bake, as is, in a medium oven. Serve with egg noodles or lentils, peas and crispy seaweed.

## Donald's Duck in Soy Sauce with Ginger – Geoffrey Donald

This is an Anglicised version of a Chinese method of cooking duck. It should have a definite, but not strong, flavour of soy and ginger, but do not over-do them.

Most supermarkets now stock tinned Chinese vegetables such as water chestnuts, snow peas and bean sprouts, also various mixtures for wok stir-frying. These are all suitable to accompany this dish. Follow the instructions on the packet or tin. Alternatively use mild flavoured vegetables such as sections of leek, strips of carrot or mange tout peas. These can be cooked along with the duck for its last twenty minutes or so. In this case carefully spoon off as much as possible of the duck fat from the cooking pot before tucking them alongside.

*One oven-prepared duck*
*100ml (4 fl oz) dry sherry*
*100ml (4 fl oz) dark soy sauce*
*Half a teaspoon sugar*
*Short length of root ginger, peeled and finely chopped (or half teaspoon ground ginger)*
*Vegetables (as suggested)*

To prepare the duck, cut away as much of the loose, fatty skin from around the neck as possible, remove any giblets, rinse well and drain. Place it, breast side down, in a lidded saucepan, casserole or small le Creuset, together with the giblets if desired. Add the sherry, soy sauce, ginger, the sprinkling of sugar and a cup of water to bulk out the liquid. Bring to the boil on a hot plate and then simmer gently for half an hour. Turn the duck over and simmer for another hour. Baste frequently so that the flavours can penetrate the flesh and also spoon off excess fat as it renders out of the body, but do not allow the liquids to reduce too much. Finally, now is the time to add any vegetables you want to cook along with the duck for the further twenty minutes or so until all is tender. In the meantime cook any other chosen vegetables, stir-fry, fried rice or egg noodles ready to serve quickly with the hot duck. Separate off any fat and use the liquid as a sauce.

## Quack-Quack – Janet Darcy

Serves two.

*2 duckling portions*
*1 medium onion*
*1-2 sticks celery*
*10 dried apricots, roughly chopped*
*40g (1½ oz) sultanas*
*Chicken stock*
*Oil*
*Salt and pepper*
*Cornflour and a little milk*

Lightly fry the chopped onion and celery in some oil. Do not colour. Add apricots, sultanas and seasonings to taste. Remove from pan and put in an ovenproof dish. Lightly fry the duck on both sides and lay on top of the contents of the dish. Have the stock hot. Cover the duck with it and put in the oven with the lid on for about an hour, until cooked. Check carefully. Mix about a heaped dessertspoon of cornflour in a little milk to a smooth paste. Remove the duck and keep hot. Add the cornflour to the juices and stir and cook until it thickens. Serve with a green vegetable and potatoes.

## Duck Breasts with Blueberries and Sloe Gin – Tidal Favourites

There are two schools of thought about fruit with duck: you either love it or hate it. In the same vein you either consider the whole point of duck to be the crispy skin, or you will enjoy the wetter dish that results from braising. I love them all, especially the contrasting sharpness and sweetness of the berries and the booze in this dish. The related cranberries also work well, and are sometimes easier to find than their cousins.

Serves four.

*4 duck breasts*
*1 chopped onion*
*1 clove chopped garlic*
*Olive oil for frying*
*Sea salt and black pepper*
*1x200g pack of blueberries*
*2 or 3 bay leaves*
*½ bottle of sloe gin, or red wine with a dash of it, or port, sherry or Madeira*
*Crème fraîche*

In Dorset, sloes abound, so it is easy for us to prick them and stick them into a bottle half-full of gin and caster sugar: after ten years it is a wonderful post-prandial drink, but it is useful for cooking any time. If you are using red wine without the sweet sloe gin you may need to add a little brown sugar or honey, to cut the sharpness of the berries.

Soften the onion and garlic in a little oil and add the duck breasts. Lightly brown them on all sides, season them, and add the blueberries, bayleaves and the booze. Cover and bring to simmer. Put in the oven at 180C (350F) for about half an hour, until the duck is tender. Remove the breasts and either keep them warm or crisp up the skin under a hot grill for a few moments. Meanwhile taste and season the sauce they cooked in and finish with crème fraîche. If you feed people who don't officially approve of sloe gin (other than for medical or religious reasons) don't tell them, and they'll never know what it is that makes the duck so succulent and flavourful…

## Peppered Duck – Philip Rudd

This is a derivative of the world famous peppered steak or Steak au Poivre. The duck breast is strong enough in flavour and texture to be able to hold the pepper and Brandy and not be swamped by it. It is particularly good served with fresh spinach and wild mushrooms.

*Two large duck breasts with the skin still on*
*Whole green peppercorns*
*Crushed Black pepper*
*Brandy*
*Cream*
*Butter*
*Wild Mushrooms*
*Fresh Spinach*
*New Potatoes*
*Chives*

### Preparation

Take the duck breasts and rub thoroughly with the crushed black pepper. If you lightly score the skin and underside of the breast you will be able to get the pepper thoroughly in. Pick and clean the spinach and wash the new potatoes.

### Cooking

Heat some butter in a frying pan. Do not over heat so as to turn the butter. Place the prepared duck breasts into the pan and cook. Allow all the juices out of the meat to mix with the butter and black pepper. Once the duck breasts are sealed, place in the oven to cook through to your own preference. Add the whole green peppercorns to the frying pan and then add a few large splashes of brandy. Burn off the alcohol. Once the alcohol is gone add the runny cream and then reduce to preferred consistency and texture. Make sure that you stir thoroughly and scrape all the juices up from the bottom of the pan. Cook the mushrooms in a little olive oil and boil off and reduce the spinach. Cook the new potatoes to your taste.

### Serving

Use a pastry cutter to place the mixed spinach and wild mushrooms on to the plate. Make sure that this mixture is thoroughly drained. (If you do not the juices from the spinach will leak into your peppered sauce). This will give you a round attractive base for the breast. Take the breast and slice into 5-7 equal portions. Using a large flat-bladed knife place across the spinach and mushroom mound. Cover the plate with the peppered sauce and garnish with chopped chives. It goes very well with a Chateauneuf du Pape.

# Turkey

## Cold Curried Turkey – Valentine Simson

Makes a lovely light supper for Boxing Day.

*About 50 g (2oz) diced cooked turkey per person*
*About 275ml (½ pint) of mayonnaise*
*1 tablespoon of Sharwoods curry sauce*
*3 tablespoons apricot jam*
*Salt and pepper*

Combine mayonnaise, salt, pepper, jam and curry sauce. Adjust the amount of apricot jam and curry sauce to taste. Carefully pour over diced turkey (or chicken) in a serving dish. Surround with cooked and cooled rice and serve with salad.

## Christmas Slurkey – Jules Monier-Williams

Go out and buy a turkey
Have a glass of whisky
Put the turkey into the oven
Have another two drinks of whisky
Set the degrees at 375 ovens
Have three more whiskers of drink
Turn oven on
Have four whisks of drinky
Turk the bastey
Whisky another bottle of get
Stick a turkey into the thermometer
Glass yourself a pour of whiskers
Bake the whisky for four hours
Take the oven out of the turkey
Take the oven out of the turkey again
Floor the turkey off the pick
Turk the carvey
Get yourself another scottle of botch
Tet the sable and pour yourself another whisk of turley
Bless the saying, pass and eat out…

## Turkey Breast, not Stuffed, but Bedded – Andrew Corran

Searching for a meal that would provide sustenance and variation for my five long-suffering children while my wife was working abroad (not lasagne again, Daddy!), I improvised this. They survived, and it became a most useful part of the repertoire. Although it requires about an hour in preparation, it has the merit that it is good either cold or re-heated next day, if there's any left… Serves eight.

*1 half breast of free range turkey, about 1.8 kg or 4 lb*
*4 large cooking apples, peeled, cored and diced*
*3 large onions, finely chopped*
*1 stick of celery, including leaves, diced*
*250g (9oz) bacon, diced*
*125g (5oz) brown (Basmati) rice*
*Good handful of cashew nuts*
*Butter*
*Sea salt and black pepper*

The preparation of the "bed" can be done well in advance, thus:

Cook the rice as instructed on the packet, or using your preferred method. This takes the longest – about forty minutes. Meanwhile, dice the bacon and cook on high heat in a frying pan in butter for about seven minutes. Remove with a slotted spoon and place in a large bowl. Cook the onion in the same pan – this may take a little longer. Add to the bowl. Now cook the celery and then the apples in the same way, tipping them into the bowl when done. Add the cooked rice and the cashew nuts and season well.

Put the rice mixture in an ovenproof dish, spread evenly and nestle the seasoned turkey breast in the middle. Cover with foil and cook in a moderate oven for about one-and-a-half-hours, removing the foil for the last twenty minutes. Slice the breast thinly and serve with its rice bed and some favourite vegetables.

# Game

## Chocolate Venison – Tidal Favourites

Winter dinner parties call for something unusual, but not too demanding on the cook. This one is best prepared the day before, as it matures nicely over twenty-four hours and only needs re-heating at the last moment. The quantities given serve twelve but can be doubled for a buffet supper, for which it is most useful, as it can easily be eaten with a fork.

*About175/200g (6/7oz) cubed lean rump venison per person*
*Olive oil for frying*
*3 large onions*
*12 cloves garlic*
*6 large carrots*
*Large punnet mushrooms*
*Red or Rosé wine, to cover meat*
*Soy and Worcester sauces, to season as liked*

Chop and fry the vegetables, in the order given, in a large ovenproof casserole. (You can vary the quantities to suit you and the season.) While they are gently cooking, sprinkle over the venison, in a large plaggy bag:

*4 tablespoons flour or cornflour*
*3 tablespoons cocoa*
*6 bayleaves*
*Lots of black pepper*
*Sea salt as liked*

When the vegetables are softened, add the seasoned venison to the casserole, and keep stirring over gentle heat until the colour of all the meat has changed. Cover with red or rosé wine, and add a good shake of soy sauce and Worcester Sauce. Bring to simmer point and cook, covered, in a low oven for two hours, or until it smells "done". Keep cool until you are ready to heat it through and adjust seasoning for serving. (Sometimes the fridge is party-full, so I have to put it outside in a box, well covered against marauding cats…)

## Fast Venison – Tidal Favourites

The quantities for this easy dish are infinitely variable. You can leave the venison marinating in the seasonings overnight in the fridge or simply sprinkle them on and stir-fry immediately. This adaptability makes it as suitable for a party as for two people. The thing to remember is that you must fry the venison strips quickly, so as not to toughen them.

> *1 steak or 175/225g (6/8oz) venison, cut into strips, per person*
> *Marinade: Madeira (enough to surround the meat), French mustard, honey, lemon juice, soy sauce, chopped ginger, Worcester sauce, Tabasco, chopped garlic, sea salt, black pepper; all more, less, or not at all, according to taste.*

Mix the marinade into the meat. Chop the following vegetables:

> *Onion(s), red, orange or yellow peppers, mushrooms*

You can use lots of vegetables or only a few. Stir-fry them in a little olive oil; leave them crisp or almost caramelise them, as you like. When you are nearly ready to serve, slip the meat with its marinade into the pan, and stir-fry until the venison changes colour. Check the seasonings and serve on rice, or with new potatoes, and a green vegetable or two. It seems to be most popular at parties if you use lots of colourful peppers to lend a festive air.

## Pheasant with Cream and Brandy – Geoffrey Donald

Here is a pheasant dish with a rich, creamy sauce, which is surprisingly easy to make. If you cannot find beef consommé, your own seasoned beef stock or dry white wine make excellent substitutes.

To serve four or so*:*

*A brace of pheasants, cleaned and prepared*
*Knob of butter*
*Four small or two large rashers of bacon*
*1 tablespoon finely chopped onion or shallot*
*A large glass of brandy*
*1 tin beef consommé*
*150ml (5oz) carton of double cream*
*Salt and black pepper*

Melt the butter in a casserole. Place the pheasants side by side in the melted butter (so that they do not stick to the bottom). Add the chopped onion round them in the butter. Add a sprinkle of salt and freshly ground black pepper and cover the breasts with a layer of the bacon. Put on the lid and cook in the oven at 220C (425F) for an hour, or until tender.

Remove from the oven, pour the brandy evenly over the birds and quickly flame it. Mix the beef consommé and the double cream; pour over the pheasants. Return to the hot oven, with the lid, and cook for a further fifteen minutes, taking care that it does not dry out or burn.

**Lulworth Castle**

## Lulworth Castle Game Pie – Sally Weld

Filling:

*1 pheasant or 3 partridges or 3 pigeons*
*450g (1 lb) minced pork*
*225g (½ lb) pork sausages or sausage-meat*
*110g (¼ lb) streaky bacon, minced*
*Minced liver from game birds (optional)*
*3 tablespoons brandy or sherry*
*Salt and ground black pepper*
*Pinch mace*
*1 clove garlic*
*1 tablespoon chopped parsley*

Pastry – French short crust:

*450g (1 lb) plain flour*
*2 egg yolks*
*225g (8oz) butter*
*2 tablespoons olive or vegetable oil*
*5/6 tablespoons cold water*

21-centimetre (8") spring form mould. Oven setting 190C (375F, gas mark 5)

**The day before:** Cut meat from birds into thin slices including legs. Place in a dish and season with salt, ground pepper and mace; pour over brandy or sherry. Cover with cling film and leave overnight.

**To prepare pastry:** Put sifted flour into a food processor with a pinch of salt. Cut butter into 8/10 pieces and process until it is the consistency of coarse breadcrumbs. With a fork lightly beat the egg yolks, oil and water. Turn on machine again and add liquid until the mixture forms a ball. Wrap in cling film and chill for approximately one hour.

**To mix the farce:** Mix pork, bacon and sausage-meat together with crushed garlic and herbs. Grease the tin and then roll out two thirds of the pastry and line the mould. Fill with alternate layers of the farce mixture and game meat, ending with the farce mixture. Roll out the remaining pastry and cover, making a small hole with a knife in the top. Decorate with pastry trimmings and brush with beaten egg.

**Baking:** Bake in the oven for approximately 35/40 minutes; lower the heat to 160C (325F, gas 3). Cover with double sheet of greaseproof paper and cook for a further 45/50 minutes. When cold remove from tin, wrap and freeze if required.

**Thawing and serving:** Allow to thaw for 24 hours. Pour in 275ml (½ pint) jellied stock through hole in centre (optional). Serve with jacket potatoes and salad. If preferred, ham or chicken can be used instead of game.

## Hambury Pheasant – Liz Rudd

One pheasant will serve about four people.

*1 pheasant*
*1 or 2 bay leaves*
*Salt and pepper*
*Parsley*
*1 large onion*
*2 sticks celery*
*2 cooking apples*
*Large knob of butter for frying*
*175ml (½ pint) cider*
*150ml (¼ pint) double cream*

Joint the pheasant as required, leaving some (perhaps the legs) on the bone. Put the carcass and giblets into a pan, to make pheasant stock, with the bay leaf, parsley and seasoning. Cover with water and simmer for an hour or two.

Peel and core the apples. Chop the celery, leaving the green leaf for decoration. Dust pheasant pieces with seasoned flour and fry in the butter in a casserole. Remove and set aside. Soften the onion, celery and apples in the butter on lower heat. Remove from heat and stir in a little flour to absorb any remaining fat. Blend in cider and 275 ml (½ pint) of the pheasant stock and simmer to reduce. Put pheasant pieces back into casserole, with more stock if needed. Season to taste. Simmer for forty-five minutes. Stir in the cream at the last moment and decorate with the celery tops as you serve each plate.

## Pheasant Pasties – Jules Monier-Williams

An excellent way to use leftover pheasant, these pasties are good for picnics, children's lunches, gamekeepers and beaters! Makes four.

*175g (6oz) cooked pheasant meat*
*100g (4oz) peeled, chopped potatoes*
*1 shallot, finely chopped*
*Mixed herbs, to taste*
*1 dessertspoon port*
*1 dessertspoon redcurrant jelly*
*225g (8oz) shortcrust pastry*
*1 egg, beaten*
*Salt and pepper*

Mix together the pheasant meat, potatoes, shallot, herbs, port, redcurrant jelly and seasoning in a bowl. Roll out pastry to ½ cm (¼ inch) thick on a floured board. Using a large saucer as a template, cut four circles. Place filling on centre of each pastry circle. Wet the edges with water, join them on top and pinch together to form frill on top. Prick with a fork. Brush pasties with beaten egg and place on a greased tray. Bake in a hot oven for ten minutes, then reduce heat to 180C (350F, gas mark 4) for a further thirty minutes.

## Pheasant with Orange and Red Wine Sauce – Jilly Palmer

Those of us with husbands or chaps that shoot often view the spoils with sinking hearts, but must remember that pound for pound the pheasant cost, in cartridges alone, the price of dinner for two in a good restaurant. Skin them rather than pluck them, to the accompaniment of some good music to put your thoughts on a higher plane... Ingredients are for eight: you need a large covered casserole dish.

*3 medium pheasants trimmed ready for cooking*
*Salt and freshly ground black pepper*
*Grated rind and flesh of one orange*
*50g (2oz) butter*
*2 tablespoons olive oil*
*2 garlic cloves, chopped*
*3 carrots, peeled and sliced*
*3 stems celery, chopped*
*Sprig of rosemary*
*570ml (1 pint) red wine*
*1 litre (1½ pints) good stock*
*25g (1oz) plain flour or cornflour*
*½ jar red currant jelly*

Season birds inside and out and rub orange peel into the skin. Cut up orange and put into the cavities of the birds.

Heat half the butter and all of the olive oil in a large pan and brown birds on all sides in the hot fat. Transfer pheasants to a plate and cook the vegetables in the remaining fat for a minute or so. Replace pheasants on to bed of vegetables and add rosemary and wine. Pour in enough stock to come halfway up the birds. Cover and simmer gently for an hour or so. When cooked, remove birds onto a serving dish and cover loosely with foil. Strain cooking liquid and make up to 570ml (1 pint) with more stock if necessary. Make buerre manie with flour and butter. Stir redcurrant jelly into hot liquid. Add buerre manie, gradually whisking to produce a smooth sauce.

Serve with simple vegetables such as boiled potatoes and sprouts.

## My Mother Said...

Welcome guests with fresh flowers, something good in the oven and open arms. Bid them goodbye by waving until they are out of sight – they will know that you are reluctant to let them go.

## Quail with Juniper Berries – Tidal Favourites

This dish originated in the need to find a game course that was not too filling for the Annual Dinner of the Cranleigh School Wine Tasting Society. The only difficult thing about it is ensuring that they are braised long enough to be tender and come away easily from the bone without falling inelegantly apart. This is much easier to manage when cooking for eight rather than for fourteen…

Quantities are **per person:**

*1 oven-ready quail*
*¼ onion, finely chopped*
*½ clove garlic, finely chopped*
*Olive oil*
*5 crushed juniper berries*
*1 bay leaf*
*1 glass white wine*
*Sea salt and black pepper*
*Crème fraîche or double cream to finish*

Soften the onion and garlic in some oil in a flameproof dish. Add the little birds and brown them gently on all sides. Add all the other ingredients except the crème fraîche and put, covered, in a moderate oven for about half an hour. Test for tenderness. Turn them so that they do not dry out. When they are done, they can cool and rest a while, breast down, until you are ready to heat them through, taste for seasoning and finish the sauce with as much crème fraîche or double cream as suits you. Purists would strain the sauce, but I prefer to remove only the bay leaves and enjoy all the other flavoursome bits as part of the sauce; that way I can rejoin the party sooner!

Note: this dish is even gamier and more intriguing if you half cover the little birds with sloe gin instead of white wine. The juniper-flavoured gin enhances the crushed berries and the sloes add a wonderful depth and plumminess. Sloes grow on our clifftops, so a good, ripe sloe gin is usually easy to obtain locally. Making it is a life-enhancing process: first you go for a windblown walk with several plastic bags to hold the blue-bloomed berries; then you prick them and drop them into a half-full bottle of gin; then you add caster sugar and shake. When the bottles are full, you screw the tops on tightly and leave on a high shelf out of temptation's way for several months. If you leave them for ten years you will have a redolent, port-like ambrosia fit for the most discerning drinker. Make it every year and this becomes a possibility, but it is so good with game, (and as an after dinner digestif,) and turns ruby red and luscious so surprisingly soon, that, in our house, it gets used before it has time to reach years of discretion…

## My Mother Said…

If a meal or a party is worth thanking your hostess for, it's worth writing – she won't want to be answering the telephone all next day, making the same responses she gave to everyone as they said their goodbyes the day before.

## Rabbit Pie – Trish Rudd

My Pa loves Rabbit Pie and by the time I was twelve years old I could skin and joint a rabbit; but that's a whole other story… There's unfortunately not much call for this dish these days, but it is a delicious alternative to Chicken Pie. Although my mother is an excellent cook, my father's Rabbit Pie is unparalleled!

*1 jointed rabbit*
*1 heaped tablespoon plain flour, seasoned with salt and pepper*
*1 medium onion, chopped*
*2-3 bacon rashers, chopped*
*4 or 5 button mushrooms, chopped (optional)*
*50g (2oz) butter*
*Mixed herbs – make sure there's lots of parsley*
*275ml (½ pint) water or stock*
*Puff or flaky pastry*

Roll rabbit in seasoned flour. (Keep the flour.) Heat half the butter in a large frying pan and gently fry the onion, mushroom and bacon. Remove these with a draining spoon when lightly cooked and fry the rabbit in the pan, turning to brown lightly on all sides. Place in an ovenproof casserole with the onion, mushroom and bacon mixture. Add herbs, salt and pepper.

Put a little more butter in the frying pan and add the remaining seasoned flour. Stir and cook over low heat until it starts to brown. Remove from heat and slowly add the stock, stirring all the time; return to heat and bring to the boil. Don't forget to stir. Pour over rabbit, cover and cook in a slow oven for two hours, or until tender. Set aside to cool.

Roll out the pastry and cover the dish to make a pie. Trim off excess pastry and make a hole in the middle to let out the steam.

If you are feeling artistic use the remaining pastry to make a pattern on the pie: a rabbit running across the top would be appropriate at Easter time, for example. Brush the top with milk, or better still with beaten egg.

Bake in pre-heated oven at about 180C (350F) for thirty to forty minutes. Serve with pride and joy!

## Rabbit with Mustard – Geoffrey Donald

Supermarkets often stock packets of cubed and frozen rabbit meat, which can conveniently be used in this recipe, though it tends to fall into smaller pieces in the cooking. However, there is no doubt that a whole animal, freshly skinned, cleaned, dismembered and chopped by your butcher has a better flavour. A mixture of two mustards is used, combining the rich taste of a brown French mustard and the sharpness of the yellow English variety. Remember that rabbit dishes are likely to contain lots of small, sharp bones!
For about four helpings:

*One rabbit, prepared as above*
*110g (4oz) bacon, lean or streaky as preferred*
*Olive oil and a knob of butter to sauté*
*A medium onion or a few shallots, chopped small*
*150ml (¼ pint) chicken stock*
*150ml (¼ pint) dry white wine*
*275ml (½ pint) double cream*
*Bouquet garni*
*Salt and black pepper*
*Teaspoon French mustard*
*Teaspoon prepared English mustard*

Cut the bacon into inch pieces and fry in a little of the oil until crisp. Transfer to a casserole. Add the butter and a little more oil to the frying pan and sauté the rabbit pieces until nicely browned before adding these to the casserole. Season with salt and pepper, add the bouquet garni and chopped onion, pour in the stock and wine, cover and simmer gently for a couple of hours or so. The supermarket rabbit meat will cook relatively quickly but an old, wild bunny may need longer to tender up… Remove the cooked rabbit pieces to a hot ovenware dish and keep warm.
Skim off the excess oil and fat, which will be floating on the surface of the sauce in the casserole, and fish out the bouquet garni. If there is too much liquid, simmer until it is reduced somewhat. Mix the two mustards into the double cream and thoroughly stir into the sauce; if you like a stronger flavour, use more mustard. Adjust the seasonings. Replace the rabbit in the casserole, cover in sauce and carefully reheat before serving with traditional vegetables.

## Three Pigeon Recipes – Yvonne Adams

### Pigeon Pie

*½ dozen or more pigeon breasts*
*2 or 3 hard boiled eggs, sliced*
*Chicken cube mixed with cup of water (or own stock)*
*1 chopped onion (optional)*
*Salt and pepper*
*Oregano*
*Flaky pastry*

A collection of china birds in the middle of the pie dish looks good.

Place breasts, seasonings and stock in an ovenproof dish. Put slices of egg on top. Cover with flaky pastry. Bake in moderate oven until pastry browns.

### Wood Pigeon Breasts

Slice down breast, and under, taking off both sides. There really is not enough flesh on the rest of the bird to bother plucking. (The offal is good cooked for your pets).

Use two halves per person. Sprinkle with seasoned salt. Sear in a hot pan with a little oil. Leave rare inside; cooking through toughens the meat too much.

Serve with pickled rock samphire and bread sauce, and/or cranberry sauce.

### Pigeon Charlotte

*2 pigeon breasts per person*
*Pluck (pigeon hearts and livers)*
*Sea salt and ground pepper*
*Herbs (thyme or oregano)*
*Bread – crumbled*
*Extra virgin olive oil*
*Glass of red wine*

Chop the pluck and season with salt and pepper. Add herbs and red wine. Roughly crumble some bread over pluck in a flat dish. Drizzle oil over breadcrumbs. Bake until the breadcrumb topping is crisp.

Cover pigeon breasts with seasoned salt and sear in a hot pan. Don't overcook or the meat will be tough – rare is best.

Pleasant served with egg noodles and baked courgettes. Slice these longways, season with oregano, salt and pepper and bake. Also good with swede mashed with salt and pepper and plenty of butter and cream, if diet allows…

# Lamb

## Portland Lamb

There is a beautiful flock of Portland sheep at Lulworth Castle. They have amazing smiley faces, and the lambs have a russet tinge to their coats. They have a good life and they make very sweet eating.

## Lamb Chops in Wine Sauce – Josie Pleavin

Cooking time about forty-five minutes. Serves four.

*25g (1oz) margarine*
*4 loin lamb chops*
*1 onion, peeled and sliced*
*1-2 teaspoons paprika*
*150ml (¼ pint) dry white wine*
*150ml (¼ pint) chicken stock*
*1 tablespoon medium sherry*
*Salt and freshly ground black pepper*
*1 teaspoon cornflour*
*50g (2oz) button mushrooms, sliced*
*2 tomatoes, skinned*
*Cream or crème fraîche, to finish*
*Chopped parsley*

Heat margarine and brown chops on each side. Drain and reserve. Add onion to pan and cook until soft, with the paprika. Allow to cool slightly and then pour on wine, stock and sherry. Return chops to pan, season well and bring to boil. Reduce heat and simmer chops, covered for about thirty minutes. Blend cornflour with a little cold water and stir into the cooking liquid, stirring all the time. Add prepared mushrooms and quartered tomatoes. Taste and adjust seasoning. Simmer for a further fifteen minutes and finish the sauce with cream if used. Place chops on a serving dish, spoon the sauce over and garnish with chopped parsley. Serve with new potatoes and buttered French beans.

## New Zealand Lamb with a Difference – Wendy Turney

Our family's favourite, very easy and very different, especially with the inclusion of pasta.

Roast:

*1 leg of lamb*

in a slow oven. About three-quarters of an hour before it is cooked, remove and pour off most of the juices.

Put in the liquidiser (double quantities for larger roast):

*1 can tomatoes*
*1 cup water*
*1 large onion, 1 clove garlic*
*1 teaspoon oregano*
*1 teaspoon sugar*
*Salt and pepper*

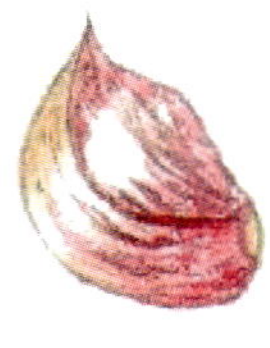

Whizz these up and pour over meat, with:

*1 large cup short macaroni*

Put back into oven to finish cooking. Serve with green salad.

## Lamb with Rosemary, Garlic and Flageolets – Suzanne Mann

Serves six.

*1. 5kg (approx.) shoulder of lamb*
*2 large cloves of garlic each cut lengthways into 8 slivers*
*1 large onion sliced thickly across*
*1 unwaxed lemon, grated rind and juice*
*1 tablespoon olive oil*
*1 tablespoon fresh rosemary needles*
*2 x 400g tins of flageolets beans*
*3 heaped tablespoons of crème fraîche*
*150ml (¼ pint) red wine*

Set the oven at 200C (400 F, gas mark 6).

Make sixteen cuts all over the shoulder and insert garlic slivers as deeply as you can. Lay the onion slices in one layer in a roasting pan, sprinkle the grated lemon rind over and sit the meat on top. Pour on the lemon juice, then oil and rosemary needles. Season. Roast for thirty minutes, then reduce heat to 150C (300F, gas 2) and continue to cook, basting occasionally, for about two and a half hours. Transfer to dish and allow to rest for ten - fifteen minutes. Meanwhile heat the beans in their liquid for about five minutes or until hot, drain and return to pan. Stir in crème fraîche and season. Put round meat. Spoon fat off roasting tin, turn up heat and deglaze with wine: reduce by half. Strain and pour over meat.

## Lecturer's Lamb – Robin Lailey via Tidal Favourites

One winter evening we were invited to attend a lecture entitled 'Heroes', organised by a friend known to us as Bearded Loony, and to have supper with him immediately afterwards. He left this casserole simmering in his oven while we listened to a most enlightening talk on Wagner, given by a friend who rejoices in the name of Vulture. Both were excellent, and so we were nourished in mind and stomach.

*1 ¾ kg (4 lb) shoulder of lamb, boned, cubed, freed of fat and gristle*
*450g (1lb) unsmoked bacon, diced*
*3 large onions, thinly sliced*
*4 tablespoons cornflour or plain flour*
*Olive oil and butter for frying*
*Sea salt and black pepper*
*2 or 3 cloves garlic, finely chopped*
*1 strip of dried or fresh orange peel*
*Juice of one large orange*
*Bouquet garni or fresh herbs as liked*
*Grated rind of one large orange, to garnish*

In a large flame-and-oven-proof casserole, fry the onions in the oil and butter until they soften; add the bacon and stir-fry while they gently brown. Shake the lamb pieces in the seasoned flour in a bag and add to the casserole, keeping them turning so that they do not burn as they change colour. Add garlic, strip of orange peel, orange juice and herbs. Put, tightly lidded, in the oven at 150C (300F) until the lecture is over. Garnish with grated rind just before serving.

## Mishmisheya – Pat Yonwin

I often make this recipe for parties – it seems to be popular, as I never have any left for next day! I like to cook casseroles in the oven; this one can be frozen and reheated when needed. Serves ten.

*3 onions*
*1½ kg (4lbs) diced lamb (Mr Blake the butcher will do it for you)*
*2 tins mixed beans or chick peas*
*Salt and pepper*
*4 teaspoons ground cinnamon*
*1kg (2½ lbs) dried apricots, cut in half*

Sauté the onion in oil until lightly browned. Add the lamb and turn to brown it. Rinse the beans and add to the meat and onions. Cover with water and bring to boil. Add seasonings and cinnamon. Cook for one and a quarter hours at 190C (375F, gas mark 5) stirring from time to time. Add the apricots and cook for a further three quarters of an hour.

## Unorthodox Moussaka – Tidal Favourites

You need to allow about 45 minutes for making this layered dish, but it is well worth the trouble and excellent invalid food. You need, **per person**:

*110g (¼ lb) best minced lamb*
*½ or ¼ chopped onion*
*½ or ¼ chopped red pepper*
*1 clove chopped garlic*
*¼ inch chopped peeled ginger root*
*½ an aubergine*
*Red wine*
*Olive oil for frying*
*Salt, pepper, Worcester sauce, Tabasco, bay leaves, rosemary.*

Soften all the chopped vegetables in a little oil; add the lamb and seasonings. Stir until the lamb changes colour on a medium heat. When all is bubbling nicely, pour enough red wine to cover the meat and leave to simmer while you do the next two steps. Fry about half an aubergine per person in olive oil, cut in ¼ inch slices. It absorbs oil at this stage and gives it back later, so be careful not to overdo the oil; a non-stick frying pan helps. Use medium heat, turn often. Season with salt and pepper. Set aside. Make a cheese sauce. Use your own recipe, or:

*Butter (about ¼ of a 250g pack)*
*Flour or cornflour (about 2 dessertspoons)*
*Milk (probably a pint)*
*Grated cheese (175g, 6oz, or more) + a further 50g, (2oz) or so for topping*
*Salt and pepper*

Quantities can vary both for the size of the meal you are making and for sloppiness; this is a very flexible dish. Melt the butter, shake in the flour, stir and bubble the roux. Pour in the cold milk all at once and stir like crazy. It needs to be quite thin when it boils, as the cheese will thicken it. When the cheese has melted into the sauce and all is smooth and glossy, pour a thin layer into the bottom of an ovenproof dish. This will receive the first layer of the fried aubergine slices. Add a layer of the meat sauce. Continue layering in this way. Finally, put a layer of sliced potatoes on top, season with salt and pepper and finish with a generous quantity of grated cheese. The potato layer is the unorthodox bit and can be left out, finishing only with the grated cheese. However, for an all-in-one dish it provides a full and satisfying meal. Bake it at 180C (350F) for an hour or so, or two hours at a lower heat. It can be served on its own or with a tossed salad, or a green vegetable.

## Spanish Lamb with Golden Cheese Shapes – Bridget Hine

The old lady who gave me this recipe was an elderly resident of a retirement home in Canberra, Australia. She had brought up a large family and was renowned for her cooking.

*700g (1-1½ lbs) of leg chops*
*110g (¼ lb) bacon rashers*
*1 tablespoon fat*
*2 tablespoons flour (seasoned with pepper and salt)*
*1 onion*
*¾ cup cubed celery*
*¾ cup green peas*
*1 teaspoon sugar*
*1 tablespoon lemon juice*
*½ cup water*
*1½ cups tomato purée*
*1 dessertspoon Worcester sauce*
*½ teaspoon salt*
*1 pinch cayenne pepper*

Trim chops, coat with seasoned flour. Fry lightly in hot fat. Remove chops; add coarsely chopped bacon and peeled sliced onion. Cook until tender. Place chops in greased casserole; add bacon and onion. Mix sugar and salt with balance of flour and sprinkle over chops. Add lemon juice, Worcester sauce and water to tomato purée and pour into casserole dish. Cover and cook in moderate oven at 190C (375F, gas mark 5) 1-¼ hours. Add peas and celery and cook for a further 30 to 35 minutes. Serve piping hot, topped with golden cheese shapes.

## Golden Cheese Shapes

Sift:

*50g (2oz) plain flour*
*75g (3oz) self-raising flour*
*1 pinch salt and cayenne pepper*

Rub in:

*75g (3oz) good shortening*

Add:

*75g (3oz) grated cheese*

Mix to a stiff dough with:

*1 egg yolk beaten with squeeze of lemon juice and 1 tablespoon of water*

Knead lightly on a floured board and roll to ¼ inch (5mm) thickness. Cut into shapes, glaze with *egg white,* sprinkle with *extra grated cheese* and *a dusting of cayenne pepper.* Bake in hot oven at 230C (450F or gas mark 8) for 7 – 10 minutes until lightly browned.

## My Mother Said…

When your husband comes home from work, feed him quickly; then he'll be receptive as a lamb to whatever you want him to do. (This used to be known as "feed the brute quickly", which is entirely inappropriate for today…)

## Stir-fry Lamb with Aubergine and Ginger – Tidal Favourites

Anything stir-fry is always quick to cook: little longer than chopping the vegetables, in fact. Have your butcher bone and cube a leg of lamb. (Dorset Lamb if possible!) Half of it will serve at least four; you can always freeze the rest against a future occasion, or use the whole leg and double up the other ingredients to serve eight. This is one you can spice up for your most adventurous diners or tone down to be sedate enough for Great Aunt Maude.

*Olive oil for frying*
*1 large onion, chopped*
*1 red, yellow or orange pepper, chopped*
*2 cloves garlic, finely chopped*
*1 large or 2 medium-sized aubergines, sliced and cubed*
*A thumb's length or so of peeled, finely chopped ginger, depending on how adventurous is Great Aunt Maude (don't grate her in!)*
*Half a boned cubed leg of lamb*
*A good sprinkle of soy sauce, Tabasco, ginger sauce, Worcester sauce and peri-peri (how much of each, if any, depending, again, on G A M)*
*Juice of ½ a lime*
*Lots of twists of the pepper mill*
*A good splash of Madeira or something similar of which G A M would approve*

A large wok-type pan is easiest to use, for speed, but any big pan will work. Start by softening the onion in the oil and add the other ingredients in the order given, stirring and turning all the time. (You will either need to chop the veg in advance, or develop four hands, or enlist Great Aunt Maude to help, as everything cooks very quickly on high heat). The lamb will only need a couple of minutes before you splash in the Madeira and serve immediately. Hopefully someone else will have organised rice or new potatoes and a fresh green vegetable to accompany it: Great Aunt Maude, maybe?

## Pork

**Piglets at Rectory Farm, Winfrith Newburgh**

There they were, snuggled up in straw in their shelter, quite irresistible; soon they were out in the open, growing fast. Happy pigs eat best…

## Bacon Chops in Cider and Orange Juice – Josie Pleavin

Quick and easy, this dish takes about five minutes to prepare and thirty to cook. Serves four.

*4 bacon chops*
*Black pepper*
*25g (1oz) margarine*
*1 small onion, peeled and finely chopped*
*150ml (¼ pint) dry cider*
*1 teaspoon sugar*
*Finely grated rind of ½ an orange*
*2 tablespoons orange juice*
*1 teaspoon cornflour*

Soak chops in cold water for two hours. Season them with freshly ground black pepper. Heat margarine and fry chops on both sides until lightly browned. Remove from pan and reserve. Fry onion until soft. Add cider to the pan with the sugar, orange rind and juice. Return chops to the pan, bring to the boil, cover and reduce heat. Allow to simmer gently for about thirty minutes. Blend cornflour with a little cold water, stir into the cooking liquid and bring to the boil, stirring. Taste and adjust seasoning. Place chops on a serving dish, spoon the sauce over and garnish with orange slices. Serve with savoury rice or duchess potatoes and peas.

## Pork Valentine – The Weld Arms, East Lulworth

Quantities are per person.

*175-225g (6-8oz) pork Valentine steak*
*1 teaspoon coarse-grain mustard*
*½ teaspoon crushed garlic*
*1 glass white wine*
*1 cup double cream*

Pan fry pork in a little oil until cooked; place under a grill on low heat to rest. Drain off the oil and return pan to heat. Add the mustard and garlic, then the wine and reduce. Add the cream and reduce again. Place pork in the sauce while it is reducing down. Place pork onto plates and pour the sauce over. Serve with fresh vegetables and potatoes of your choice.

## Grandmother's Remedies – Sally Lee

**Asthma:** Roll a spider's web into a ball and swallow it!

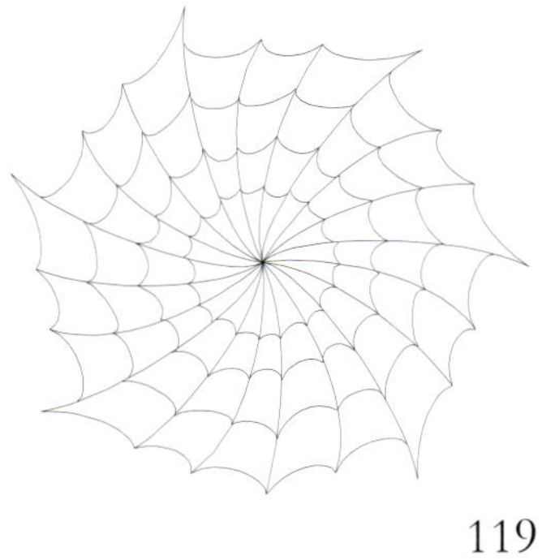

## Pork with Gruyere – Andrew Corran

Being married to a superb cook, I found opportunities to impress with my modest culinary skills very limited, and the inclination to do so almost non-existent. However, one evening when she was too tired to do other than collapse with a glass or two of wine, I adapted a recipe from a high-powered cookbook to my lazy ways. The result has become a family favourite: it is simple and quick to do – and distinctly rich…
Serves four.

*4 thickish pork loin steaks (or chops)*
*450g (1 lb) Gruyère cheese*
*3 tablespoons Meaux mustard (I prefer the whole grain Pommery)*
*Olive oil*
*Butter*
*Garlic (optional - I cheat with garlic purée)*
*Salt and freshly ground black pepper*
*275ml (½ pint) double cream or crème fraîche*

Trim excess fat from pork pieces and fry them in the butter and olive oil. Season to taste. Grate the cheese into a bowl. Add the mustard, cream, (garlic) and mix together to make a gooey paste. Spread this (with any surplus pan scrapings mixed in) on the pork pieces and grill until golden brown. Spoon the grill-pan drippings over the meat and serve with new potatoes and vegetables as available. This also works well with gammon.

## Pork with Mustard, Apples and Cider – Tidal Favourites

Piggy seems to have an affinity with apples. My husband doesn't officially like smooth French mustard, but he enjoys this dish, in which all the ingredients meld together into a fragrant slosh around the pieces of pork.

For each person you need:

*1 good-sized pork chop or 2 slices of pork fillet*
*1 cooking apple*
*½ a chopped onion*
*½ an inch of chopped fresh ginger*
*A good smear of Dijon mustard*
*A drizzle of honey, especially if the apples are very sour*
*Olive oil*
*Salt, pepper, bayleaves, crushed juniper berries (optional)*
*Cider to cover*

These quantities are variable, of course, but you do need plenty of apples. It is easiest to make if you have a wide metal pan that will start the onions on the ring and will transfer to the oven when you have added all the other ingredients.

Gently cook the onions in a little oil while you peel, core and roughly chop the apples. Generously smear both sides of the pork pieces with mustard and a little honey and cook with the onions for a few minutes on each side. Add the chopped apples, ginger and seasonings, and cover with cider. Bring to simmering point and put in a low oven, covered, for about an hour. It will happily rest and reheat, or you can hurry it up in a higher oven if you are impatient for it.

## Winter Bake Hot Pot – Barbara Wilding

*135kg (3lbs) boiling potatoes*
*450g (1lb) carrots*
*450g (1lb) parsnips*
*1 small swede*
*1 large leek*
*Salt and pepper*
*25g (1oz) margarine*
*2 Oxo cubes*
*225g (8oz) bacon*
*2 garlic sausages*
*225g (8oz) grated cheese*
*225g (8oz) breadcrumbs*
*1 onion*
*Pinch of herbs (optional)*
*2 tablespoons flour*

Boil potatoes, carrots, parsnips and swede for twenty minutes. Put vegetables into casserole; reserve boiling juice for sauce. Fry chopped bacon, leek and onion in a deep frying pan until golden brown. Mix gently into vegetables. Stir thick slices of sausage into vegetables. Melt margarine in frying pan, add flour and make a roux. Add boiling juice, make up to half a pint (275ml) of sauce. Add salt and pepper to taste. Add herbs if desired. Pour over vegetables. If sauce does not cover adequately add a little water until vegetables are just covered. Mix cheese and breadcrumbs together and place over vegetables in casserole. Bake for 45 minutes in a medium oven 180C (350F, gas mark 4) until top of casserole is brown and crusty.

# Puddings and Sweet Sauces

## Apple Paradise – Jules Monier-Williams

Make the topping first:

*1 cup self-raising flour*
*1 cup soft brown sugar*
*110g (4oz) butter*
*½ teaspoon salt*
*1 teaspoon cinnamon (optional)*

Mix topping lightly with two knives or fingers until crumbly. Prepare apples.

*7-8 good cooking apples, peeled, cored and sliced*
*Sugar to taste if needed*
*Butter to dot on top*
*Grated rind and juice of a lemon*

Spread topping over apples and bake in a moderate oven until apples are cooked. Serve hot or cold.

## Apricot Cream – Jules Monier-Williams

*225g (8oz) dried apricots, soaked overnight in just under 570ml (1pint) cold water*
*Sugar to taste*
*1 tablespoon gelatine*
*150ml (¼ pint) cream, whipped*
*2 egg whites, stiffly beaten*
*Squeeze of lemon juice*

Stew apricots gently and sieve while hot. Dissolve gelatine in a little water over simmering water and add squeeze of lemon. When setting, add whipped cream and fold in stiffly beaten egg whites. Chill.

## Baked Custard – Tidal Favourites

My mother always made this as recovery food after an illness or operation; it is nourishing, comforting, and slips down easily. It is also easy to cover the ramekins with cling film and pop them in a basket to take to a friend in bed or hospital. It is good, even if you are not ill, and quick to make.

*3 eggs*
*100g (3½ oz) sugar*
*Pinch of salt*
*615ml (21fl oz) milk*
*1 teaspoon real vanilla essence*
*Freshly grated nutmeg*

Heat the milk to scalding point; don't boil. Add the vanilla and stir in the well-beaten eggs, sugar and salt. Blend well to dissolve the sugar.

Pour into buttered ramekins and grate nutmeg over the top. Set in a shallow oven tray of water and bake at 180C, 350F for about thirty to forty minutes, depending on your oven. Test by inserting a silver knife or spoon into the custard near the edge. If it comes out clean, the custard will be firm when it cools.

## Baked Lemon Pudding – Tidal Favourites

This is the lightest lemon sponge with a soft custard underneath. It is a wonderful recipe, but seems to use a million separate bowls in the making… Serves six.

Butter a 2.25 litre (4 pint) baking dish.
Sift together:

*200g (7oz) sugar*
*100g (3½ oz) plain white flour*
*½ teaspoon baking powder*
*¼ teaspoon salt*

Separate:

*3 eggs*

Beat the whites until stiff. Beat in, a spoonful at a time,

*100g (3½ oz) sugar*

Set aside. Without washing the beater, beat the yolks until light. Add:

*Grated rind and juice of one lemon*
*2 tablespoons melted butter*
*1½ cups (330ml, 12fl oz) milk*

Stir into the flour mixture. Beat until smooth.. Fold in the beaten whites. Pour into the baking dish and set into a pan of water 1 cm (½ inch) deep. Bake for about forty-five minutes at 180C (350F).

## Blueberry Clouds – Margaret Whitehouse

Blueberries are delicious when in season and refreshingly different for a party pud. It can be made in advance as it keeps well for a day or two in the fridge. Serves eight.

*250ml natural set yoghurt*
*250g (9oz) fresh blueberries*
*250ml whipping cream*
*3 tablespoons sugar*

Lightly cook the blueberries with the sugar. Take off the heat and leave to cool. Place yoghurt in the base of a glass serving dish. Pour on the blueberries when cold, reserving a few for decoration. Beat the cream until it reaches the soft peak stage and pour over the blueberries. Decorate with the remaining fruit and chill until serving time.

## Banoffee Meringue and Butterscotch Sauce – Tidal Favourites

Born out of the need to make a gluten free Banoffee Pie, I put together my grandmother's recipe for meringue and my mother's for butterscotch sauce and made them into a seriously gooey sort of Pavlova. The health-food police would rightly say it should be banned, as almost every ingredient is rich and bad for you. It is usually the first to go at parties and is the recipe I am most often asked for afterwards. Quantities are for twelve to fourteen partygoers: double for big gatherings and halve for normal ones...

Make the meringue first:

*6 egg whites (use the yolks for Hollandaise or mayonnaise)*
*375g (13oz) golden caster sugar*
*2 teaspoons real vanilla essence*

To make up:

*2 x 570ml (1 pint) cartons double cream*
*12 large ripe bananas*
*Butterscotch sauce, as much as you can pour on without overflowing...*

Beat the egg whites until foamy. Slowly beat in the sugar. Add the vanilla. Spread onto a large rice paper lined or buttered baking tray, or two smaller ones, building up the sides to contain the whipped cream, bananas and sauce. Bake in a slow oven at about 110C (230F) for up to two hours. The best Pavlova bases are crisp without and chewy within, but you can dry them right out if you want them to keep for some time. Just before the party begins, fill them with soft-whipped cream (you will need at least two large cartons) into which you have folded some of the butterscotch sauce. Slice a good thick layer of bananas onto the cream and cover generously with the cooled butterscotch sauce. Sell your guests this book when they ask for the recipe!

## Butterscotch Sauce

This, too, can be made well in advance of the party, as it needs to be cool before using. Put in a heavy saucepan:

*1x 250g pack slightly salted butter*
*500g (1 lb 2oz) dark brown molasses or Muscovado sugar*

Melt these together, stirring, until they are good and bubbly. Remove from heat and rest for a moment. (A good time to make a cup of tea.) Stir in a large carton of *double cream* (about three-quarters of a pint, but you can vary the amount.) If the mixture is still very hot it will erupt like a lava flow, but have courage and keep stirring until all is smooth and glossy. Cool before adding to the Banoffee as above.

The flavour of this rich dark brown sauce comes as a surprise to people who are expecting chocolate, and it absolutely transforms plain vanilla ice cream or sponge cake, when poured over it, either hot or cold. It keeps well in the fridge, and can be re-heated or used thick, cold and gooey.

## Butterscotch Ice Cream

For a sumptuously smooth and wicked ice cream, gently fold some of the cooled sauce into soft-whipped double cream. It is all too easy to turn it into a sort of separated butter if you use the electric beater, so go carefully! Use quantities to suit your taste for more or less butterscotch flavour. Freeze: allow to soften for twenty minutes or so before serving.

## Brambles

Blackberries grow well in Dorset. There is little to beat picking the ones that grow on our clifftops, with the warm September sun bringing out the scent, and the prospect of capturing some of the essence of a Lulworth summer for winter use. They are wonderful when stewed with sugar, frozen, and reheated to be served with yogurt or cream as a simple winter pud. They are equally good in pies, or made into jellies and jam. These two recipes are unusual, and very decorative for a dinner party.

### Blackberry Sherbet – Audrey Parson

*1½ -2 cups blackberries or any soft fruit*
*1 cup sugar*
*¾ tablespoon gelatine*
*2 tablespoons cold water*
*2 tablespoons hot water*
*1 tablespoon lemon juice*
*2-3 tablespoons double cream*
*2 egg whites*

Sprinkle gelatine onto the cold water, add the hot water and dissolve over a saucepan of simmering water. Mix fruit and sugar and allow to stand for a while. When gelatine is cool add to fruit together with the lemon juice. Put in fridge until about to set, then whisk until it is fluffy and fills a large bowl. Fold in the whipped cream and beaten egg whites. Chill again until it slightly sets.

### Blackberry Bombe – Elizabeth Megahey

*450g (1 lb) blackberries*
*110g (4oz) sugar*
*1 tablespoon water*
*150ml (¼ pint) double cream*
*150ml (¼ pint) single cream*
*75g (3oz) broken meringues*

Make purée with blackberries, sugar and water. Whip creams together until they just hold shape and fold in meringue pieces. Add half of the purée and carefully fold in – do not overfold, as the mixture should have a marbled appearance. Turn into a 1.2 litre (2 pint) pudding basin, smooth the surface, cover and freeze. When serving, stand the frozen bowl in hot water for a few seconds, turn out the bombe and spoon a little of the reserved purée over it. Serve the rest separately.

## Bread and Butter Pudding – Gwen Walsh

The easy way…

*1 rich fruit loaf, sliced if possible*
*110g (4oz) mixed dried fruit*
*Marmalade*
*2 medium eggs*
*425ml (¾ pint) milk*
*½ teaspoon cinnamon, if liked*

Spread marmalade over fruit loaf slices and then cut into quarters. Layer into an ovenproof dish, spreading the dried fruit onto each layer, but not on the top. Beat the egg and milk together and gently pour over. Leave to stand for half an hour. Sprinkle cinnamon over the top before baking in a medium hot oven for thirty to forty minutes, until golden brown on top.

## Heavenly Hash – Gwen Walsh

If red maraschino cherries are not available, a small tub of cake cherries will do. Likewise, if soured cream is unobtainable, use fresh cream soured with one tablespoon of lemon juice.

*1 small tin mandarin segments*
*1 bottle red maraschino cherries*
*1 small tin pineapple pieces*
*1 small packet each of white and pink marshmallows, or one large mixed pack*
*1¼ cups soured cream*
*Pinch ground cardamom*
*¼ teaspoon ground ginger*
*1 teaspoon grated orange rind*
*1 tablespoon Cointreau (optional)*

Drain fruit; halve cherries and marshmallows. Toss carefully together in a large bowl. Whip sour cream with remaining ingredients. Fold cream mixture through fruit and marshmallows. Chill for about one to two hours, until serving time.

## Grape Crème Brulée – Jilly Palmer

It is better not to put this into the fridge after the sugar is caramelised, as it may go soggy, but it can be prepared well in advance. Serves six to eight.

*900g (2 lbs) grapes, preferably seedless*
*275ml (½ pint) double cream or half and half cream and Greek yoghurt or Crème fraîche*
*110g (4oz) caster sugar*

Be sure that you make this in an ovenproof dish which is not too deep to slip under the grill. Place grapes in dish. Whip cream or cream mixture stiffly and smooth over the grapes. (Any fruit mixture, fresh or tinned may be used, of course.) Place dish in the freezer for two or three hours. Remove and spread caster sugar thickly over the whole surface. Slide under very hot grill until sugar caramelises.

## Chocolate Fudge Pudding – Tidal Favourites

This rich, black fudge cake with its own sauce underneath is truly awesome in its chocolatey-ness. It is most definitely not for slimmers, or the faint-hearted.

Sift together:

*¾ cup (175g, 6oz) granulated sugar*
*1 cup (145g, 5oz) plain flour*
*2 teaspoons baking powder*
*½ teaspoon salt*

Melt together in a saucepan:

*¼ pack (50g, 2oz) butter*
*3 tablespoons cocoa*

Add to the flour mixture. Stir in:

*½ cup (110ml, 4fl oz) milk*
*1 teaspoon real vanilla essence*

Pour into a buttered baking dish about 75 cm (9ins) square. Over the top, scatter, without mixing:

*½ cup (110g, 4oz) dark brown sugar*
*½ cup (110g, 4oz) granulated sugar*
*4 tablespoons cocoa (heaped for chocoholics)*
*1½ cups (330ml, 12fl oz) strong cold coffee*

Bake for about 30-35 minutes at 180C (350F). Be careful not to overbake, as the cake should be fudgey and the sauce gooey. Serve warm, with cream or plain ice cream. They will hardly be able to rise from their chairs, but they will ask for it again and again.

## Easy Honeycomb Whip – Chris Cobb

Serves four.

*1 packet of raspberry or strawberry jelly*
*150ml (¼ pint) water*
*275ml (½ pint) milk*
*2 eggs, separated*
*1 level tablespoon sugar*
*Grapes to decorate (if liked)*

Make jelly in hot water (not boiling). Beat egg yolks with milk, then stir into jelly; cool. Whip egg whites stiff and add sugar; whisk again. Add a quarter of the jelly mixture, whisk, and fold in the rest of the jelly.

## Chocolate Roulade – Anne Smith

This delicious recipe has been a favourite of mine for many years and is kept for special occasions. Small portions are the order of the day as it is very rich and gooey, but it makes a very impressive dinner party pudding which always seems to go down well with my guests. I make it the evening before it is to be served, leaving it in the tin in the fridge until late the next day, when I add the filling, which cuts down on the workload on the day I am entertaining.

*175g (6oz) good quality plain chocolate*
*5 eggs*
*225g (8oz) caster sugar*
*3 tablespoons water*

Line a shallow Swiss roll tin 30 x 20 cm (12 x 8 inches) with oiled greaseproof paper. Separate the eggs and gradually add the yolks to the caster sugar in a big bowl, beating until the mixture is pale lemon in colour; add the water and stir well. Melt the chocolate in a bowl over a small saucepan of simmering water until thick and creamy. Remove from the heat but keep the bowl over the pan of water. Beat the egg white to form a firm snow. Add the chocolate to the egg yolk mixture and stir well until the two are well blended and of uniform colour. Cut and fold the beaten whites into this and turn into prepared tin. Bake at 180C (350F) for ten to fifteen minutes until firm to the touch. Have ready a clean tea towel wrung out in cold water. Take the roulade out of the oven, leave in the tin and cool slightly before covering with the damp tea towel. Put in the fridge and leave for twelve hours or overnight.

Filling:

*275ml (½ pint) lightly whipped cream, flavoured with vanilla essence, rum or brandy*

When ready to add the filling lay a sheet of greaseproof paper on the work surface and dust well with icing sugar. Remove the cloth and turn the roulade upside-down onto the prepared paper and shake out of the tin. Remove the greaseproof paper (it will stick but gives the cook a treat scraping the leftovers off with a knife!), spread with whipped cream and roll up like a Swiss roll. It will crack and look messy at this stage but don't worry, with a dusting of icing sugar applied before serving on a pretty plate it will look really good.

## My Mother Said…

Always put a pinch of salt in everything, even sweet things. It brings out the flavour.

## Coconut Ice Cream and Lime Syrup – Wendy Turney

Mix together:

*3 egg yolks*
*1 teaspoon cornflour*
*1 teaspoon vanilla extract*

Combine:

*570ml (1 pint) milk*
*5 tablespoons instant coconut powder*

Heat and whisk. Pour into the egg mixture, put back onto heat and whisk until it thickens. When custard is cold add:

*75ml (3 fl oz) whipping cream*

Half freeze this mixture and then whip all up and freeze again.

I usually make **Lime Syrup** to go with this:

*Lime juice*
*Water*
*Sugar*

Use quantities to suit and thicken with a little *arrowroot.*

## Deborah's Apple Pudding – Jilly Palmer

Its inventor reckons this scrumptious pudding will serve four "greedies" or six normal people. It is very useful to offer to people who cannot eat wheat flour.

*900g (2 lbs) cooking apples (English, of course)*
*25g (1oz) butter*
*110g (4oz) brown sugar*
*Cinnamon stick or powdered cinnamon to taste*

Soften apples with brown sugar and stir in the butter. Remove cinnamon stick after cooking.

Topping:

*110g (4oz) ground almonds*
*110g (4oz) sugar*
*110g (4oz) butter*
*2 large eggs, beaten*

Cream butter and sugar until pale; gradually add the eggs. Slowly stir in the ground almonds and mix well. Put apple in ovenproof dish and smooth over the topping. Bake at 180C (350F, gas mark 4) for about three quarters of an hour. The top will be dark when done. Serve with lots of thick pouring cream.

## French Creams – Tidal Favourites

One time when we were on holiday in France, we were teasing a friend about wearing his late mother's diamanté-trimmed spectacles instead of stretching the budget to a more appropriate pair. Taking them off to make a pontifical point in response, he dropped them in the crème-fraîche he was eating at the time. He did not enjoy our helpless laughter very much, but has since enjoyed this version of the dish at almost every dinner party…

Quantities are variable, according to the size of the party, and they can be made the day before.

*Equal quantities double cream and plain yogurt*
*Caster sugar to taste*
*Real vanilla essence, to taste*
*Dark soft brown Barbados or molasses sugar*

Soft-whip the cream, yogurt, sugar and vanilla together. Don't over-whip, as the mixture stiffens in the fridge. Spoon carefully into glasses and generously cover with brown sugar. Chill.

## Heather Flan – Josie Pleavin

*2 packets Almond Shortbread Biscuits*
*25g (1oz) chopped walnuts*
*½ teaspoon ground cinnamon*
*150g (5oz) unsalted butter (melted)*

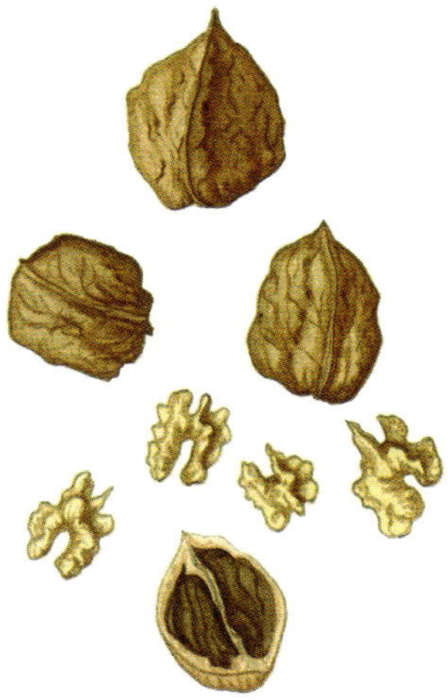

**Filling:**

*450g (1lb) fresh raspberries*
*100g (4oz) blueberries*
*300ml (½ pint) double cream*
*150ml (¼ pint) soured cream*
*1 tablespoon caster sugar*
*1 tablespoon brown sugar*

Grease a 25cm (10-inch) loose-bottomed flan tin, flan ring or dish. Crush shortbreads in food processor or polythene bag. Mix walnuts, cinnamon and melted butter and add to shortbread crumbs. Press firmly onto base and up the sides of the container. Refrigerate for at least one hour. Carefully place biscuit base onto plate and scatter half the fruit over. Whip double cream until it stands in soft peaks. Stir in soured cream and caster sugar. Spoon over the berries. Scatter the remainder of the berries over the cream and sprinkle with brown sugar. Serve immediately.

## Granny Mees' Meringues or Pavlova Base – Tidal Favourites

*4 large egg whites*
*1¼ cups (250g, 9oz) caster sugar*
*1 teaspoon real vanilla essence*
*Pinch salt*

Free-range eggs make the best meringues and the easiest conscience. Beat the whites until stiff and then beat in the sugar, vanilla and salt. (My mother said you should always put a smidgen of salt into *everything.)* For Pavlova bases, smooth into two shallow round baking trays, buttered, or one party-sized oblong one. For individual meringues, drop from a spoon, (large, medium or small,) onto a buttered baking tray. Bake in a low oven 1½ to 2 hours. The nicest meringues are crisp without and chewy within.

Individual meringues can be put together with whipped cream and served with stewed fruit or fool; or with **Chocolate Sauce**, or with **White Chocolate Mocha Sauce.** Or you can be really wicked with a sinful **Ganache** made from equal parts of *melted dark chocolate, butter and whipped cream.* Build the meringues into a mountain with this, betwixt, between, above, below, and licence their roving spoons to go…

## Fruity Pavlova

Fill the meringue cases with slightly sweetened softly whipped double cream, layered with any soft fruit of your choice. Strawberries and raspberries are always popular, or nectarines and peaches are good in season. So are ripe and juicy pears, stewed, sweetened and cinnamon-enriched cooking apples, stewed and sweetened cranberries or blueberries, or, indeed, any fruit that takes your fancy from the garden or the supermarket shelves… Save a few choice fruits for decoration. Put candles on it and it makes a good gluten-free birthday cake.

## Hot Chocolate Sauce and Chocolate Ice Cream – Tidal Favourites

If you cook this seriously chocolatey sauce for longer than its allotted three minutes it becomes progressively more toffee-like. Children of all ages adore it solidifying chewily over ice cream. If you really want toffee, cook it for ten minutes, or until a drop sets on a saucer, pour it into a flat baking tray and mark it into squares as it cools. Otherwise, it makes an excellent topping for anything from cakes to profiteroles, and, of course, ice cream.

Put into a heavy saucepan:

*1/3 cup (75ml, 3fl oz) water*
*2 heaped tablespoons cocoa*
*2 tablespoons golden syrup*
*1 cup (200g, 7oz) sugar*
*A dollop of butter (about dessertspoon size)*
*Pinch salt*

Stir and bring to boil. Bubble for three minutes. Cool slightly and add:

*1 teaspoon vanilla*

## Chocolate Ice Cream

For the smoothest, chocolatiest ice cream, that beats even the best commercial ones, simply fold the cooled sauce into 600ml (20fl oz or two standard cartons) of softly whipped double cream, and freeze. You can vary the proportions of sauce to cream for a more or less chocolatey ice cream. Be careful not to over beat, or it can separate. Take it out of the freezer to soften slightly about 20 minutes before serving.

## Mint Ice Cream – Jean Moxham

If, like me, you enjoy the lovely scent of mint leaves from the garden, you will like the unusual, delicate flavour of this recipe. I think that dark chocolate, either made into a sauce and poured over, or grated on top before serving, might be nice.

*225g (8oz) caster sugar*
*275ml (1/2 pint) water*
*2 teacups mint leaves stripped from the stem*
*Juice of 1 lemon*
*275ml (1/2 pint) double cream*

Measure the sugar and water into a saucepan and stir over low heat to dissolve sugar. Bring to boil and simmer for one minute, then draw off heat and let the syrup cool. Put the mint leaves into a blender and pour in the cold syrup. Cover with lid and blend for a few seconds until the mint is very finely chopped. Pour syrup through a nylon sieve into a mixing bowl to strain off the leaves. Add the lemon juice to the syrup. Soft-whip the cream and fold into the syrup.

Pour the mixture into a freezer container and freeze uncovered until it is partially frozen. Turn into a chilled bowl and whisk until smooth. Return to the freezer container immediately and freeze for several hours without stirring, until firm. Transfer to the fridge for thirty minutes to allow it to soften slightly before serving. Decorate with mint leaves.

## Kahlufle – Tidal Favourites

Born of a certain desperation to find a pudding for the third dinner of a weekend house party that all of a fussy lot would like, this take on Tiramisu/Real Trifle turned out to be a winner. The subtle coffee flavour of the sponge and custard is made even more luscious by the Kahlua or Tia Maria, but Madeira or brandy is pretty good, too. Serves about sixteen people, depending on the size of your glasses, or eight greedy pigs who come back for seconds. Start with the sponge.

### Coffee Sponge Cake

Separate:

*5 eggs (free-range if possible)*

Beat the whites until foamy and slowly add:

*¼ cup (50g, 2oz) golden caster sugar*

In another bowl, beat yolks with:

*¼ cup (55ml, 2fl oz) strong black coffee*

When thick, gradually beat in:

*¾ cup (150g, 5oz) golden caster sugar*

Gently fold the whites into the yolks. Sift together and fold in:

*1 cup (150g, 5oz) plain white flour*
*¼ teaspoon salt*

Pour into three unbuttered shallow cake tins (preferably with rotating sliders to release cakes) or one large springform tin. Bake at 180C, 350F for 10 to 20 minutes, or until it bounces back from a quick finger prod. While the sponge is baking, make the custard.

### Coffee Custard

Put into a heavy (non stick) saucepan:

*6 (free-range) eggs,*
*1 cup (230g, 8oz) golden caster sugar*
*3 teaspoons real vanilla essence*
*570ml (1 pint) double cream*
*275 ml (½ pint) strong black coffee*

Whisk all together. Now you need patience. Stirring firmly (a flat-bottomed slotted wooden implement is best for this) right across the bottom of the whole pan, slowly bring the custard to blood heat. Test this with your finger; when it is too hot to bear you are nearly there. Continue to stir until the custard thinly coats the back of a silver spoon.

*Kahlua, Tia Maria, Madeira or brandy, to soak the sponge*

When the sponge cakes spring back to the finger test, remove from their tins and cool on a wire rack. Break them into bits and half-fill sundae or wineglasses with the pieces. Pour Kahlua or Tia Maria over the sponge pieces as generously as you like and then pour your coffee custard over them to an elegant depth. There is no need to gild such a rich lily, but a layer of whipped cream on top, sprinkled with cocoa or best chocolate powder or plain chocolate shavings, will prevent the custard forming a skin and make it even more of a party pud.

It can be served, trifle-style, as whole, booze-soaked cakes, covered with the coffee custard, whipped cream and whatever decoration you fancy. Walnuts, pecans or crushed roasted hazel nuts are good, as well as chocolatey things.

## Lemon Fluff – Mariane Thompson

This is very easy and fresh and goes well after a rich main course. Serves four to six.

*4 eggs, separated*
*4 tablespoons granulated sugar*
*1 lemon, grated rind and juice*
*2 tablespoons icing sugar*
*2 tablespoons hot water*

In a bowl mix egg yolks and granulated sugar, plus finely grated rind and juice of the lemon and two tablespoons of water. Stir gently until the mixture thickens over a pan of simmering water. Remove from the heat and fold in the whites that have been stiffly beaten with the icing sugar. Spoon into glass dishes and put into the fridge to cool.

## Lemon Grape Brulée – Liz Rudd

The wickedness of the Port, sugar and cream is offset by the refreshing tang of the grapes and the crunch of the brulée, making this a popular party pudding. It keeps well in the fridge. Serves eight.

*1 packet of lemon jelly*
*275 ml (½ pint) water*
*225g (½ lb) seedless grapes*
*½ cup Port to make up liquid to 430ml (¾ pint)*
*570ml (1pint) double cream*
*Demerara sugar*

Dissolve the jelly in the water and port (in proportions to please your more or less boozy guests.) Split grapes in half and put in a shallow ovenproof dish. Pour jelly over and put in the fridge to set. Whip cream until thick and spread over the set jelly. Cover thickly all over with the demerara sugar. Heat a grill to high temperature. Meanwhile place the dish in another container holding cold water to prevent the jelly melting, and put under the grill until the sugar melts and caramelises. Chill until serving time.

## Orange Bombay – Jane Pickton

You can easily adjust quantities to serve the numbers you have to feed.

*Swiss roll with jam, or some similar cake, such as cherry sponge, (bought or make your own) with no cream or vanilla.*
*Brandy*
*Tin of mandarin oranges*
*Custard (tin, powder or make your own). It needs to set.*
*1 – 3 egg whites for making meringue*

In a large serving bowl slice the cake and cover the bottom. (Of the bowl!) Poor over enough Brandy that you are comfortable with plus the juice from the tinned oranges. Arrange the oranges on top. Make a thick custard and before it sets (i.e. it's still warm) pour on top. Now whisk the egg whites until little mountains can be made. Put this on top of the custard. Heat the grill and pop it under so that the egg whites just brown. Serve immediately.

Note: Egg yolks can be used for a Béarnaise sauce with a good fillet steak, but that's when the children are away!

## Lemon Ice Cream – Tidal Favourites
### Especially for Olivia Travers

This Coast and Country Cooking book has been a long time a-making. I had tucked this recipe into a page of lemony puds, and given it to a young pianist friend of ours to proofread. Olivia's entries in our visitor's book always feature the ice creams she has eaten during her stay, but I hadn't realised what a complete glaceophile she really is until she insisted that my mother's Lemon Ice Cream have a page to itself, arrowed, starred and shouting: "This is the reason I'm buying this book!" Such a reaction is immensely flattering, considering that this is the simplest ice cream you could ever hope to find. You can even mix it in the bowl you intend to freeze and serve it in.

*Grated rind and juice of 2 unwaxed lemons*
*1 tablespoon of runny honey*
*Sugar to take up the juice*
*570ml (1 pint) cream (double, single, or a mixture)*

Mix together, cover with cling film and freeze. No need to stir halfway through freezing, but take out to thaw for at least twenty minutes before serving.

It's a wonderful standby for the freezer and mixes well with other puds at a party, when greedy pigs like me want to try everything.

## Lemon Surprise – Susan Marsh

On our return to England from touring round the Continent, we discovered Casa Pizza along the towpath in Richmond, Surrey. The chef used to throw pizza dough around in order to shape it, much to the amusement of the children. We spent many a happy hour there with friends. On one memorable occasion a friend ordered a Lemon Surprise as a dessert. When it arrived the surprise was that it was an Orange! Thus the recipe, which serves six to eight…

*550ml (1 pint) water*
*225g (8oz) sugar*
*275ml (½ pint) lemon or orange juice*
*1 egg white*
*A sprinkle of liqueur (optional)*

Place water and sugar in a pan and heat over a medium heat until the sugar dissolves. Simmer gently for three minutes, leave to cool. Stir in the lemon or orange juice, pour into an ice-tray and freeze until soft and mushy, about one-two hours. Fold in whisked egg white until texture is smooth and return to ice-tray and freeze for two-three hours or overnight. To serve, the water ice should be a soft mushy texture. If it is frozen hard, allow to stand at room temperature until it softens a little. Serve in hollow lemons or oranges with a sprig of fresh mint. Sprinkle a little liqueur over the water ice before serving.

## Mango and Lemon Mousse – Tidal Favourites

Children as well as adults seem to enjoy this bright yellow party pud. The mango gives it an intriguing flavour, but you can leave it out for a simple lemon mousse. Serves eight or so.

*Grated rind and juice of 2 unwaxed lemons*
*Flesh of one mango, puréed in the blender*
*4 eggs, separated*
*105g (4oz) caster sugar (x 2)*
*1 packet gelatine, dissolved in a little cold water*
*274ml (½ pint) cream, soft whipped*

Sprinkle gelatine over cold water (about 6 tablespoons) in a basin and dissolve over a saucepan of boiling water. Beat egg yolks with 105g caster sugar until thick and creamy. Add lemon juice and rind, chobbled mango, dissolved gelatine and whipped cream. Lastly, fold in egg whites, beaten to stand up in peaks with the second 105g of caster sugar. Pour into a pretty bowl to set in the fridge, or use individual glasses or ramekins.

## Miss York's Chocolate Mousse – The Robertson Family

*225g (8oz) plain chocolate*
*2 tablespoons double cream*
*4 eggs*
*Few drops vanilla essence*

Break up the chocolate and heat in a double saucepan with the cream, stirring all the time until melted.

Separate the eggs and beat the yolks into the cooled mixture (3-5 minutes). Whip the whites until stiff and fold in.

## Mocha Mousse with Crunchy Praline – Tidal Favourites

One method of crushing the praline is to put it inside two plastic bags and stamp on it, or bash it with a rolling pin on the garden wall. If you don't crush it fine enough you run the risk of having a rude friend like one of ours enquire what these lumps of concrete are… On the other hand, too fine and it will sog, not crunch. However, it is worth the trouble, as it is always one of the first to go at parties.

Praline:

*25g (1oz) flaked almonds*
*25g (1oz) caster sugar*
*(You can make more if you want extra crunch)*

Place almonds and sugar in a heavy pan and dissolve sugar very slowly over heat. As the sugar browns, stir mixture so almonds are toasted. When browned, turn onto a buttered plate. Crush when cold.

Mousse:

*4 eggs, separated*
*110g (4oz) caster sugar*
*2 dessertspoons instant (de-caf) coffee*
*2 dessertspoons cocoa dissolved in 6 tablespoons boiling water*
*10g (½ oz) gelatine dissolved in 5tablespoons cold water over boiling water*
*284ml (10fl oz) double cream*

Dissolve the coffee granules and cocoa in the boiling water. Put egg yolks, sugar and coffee/chocolate mixture in a bowl and whisk until thick and mousse-like. Lightly whip cream and fold 2/3 of it into mixture. Soak gelatine in a bowl in the cold water over a saucepan of boiling water until dissolved. Add to mixture. Whip egg whites until stiff and fold into soufflé mixture. Stir carefully until it thickens a little and then put into a pretty dish. A cut glass bowl or 6" soufflé dish does well. Put in fridge to set and when quite firm, cover with remaining soft-whipped cream and crushed praline.

## Mrs Michael's Pudding – The Robertson Family

An old-fashioned steamed pudding – a family favourite for Sunday Lunch in the winter.

*110g (4oz) flour*
*110g (4oz) breadcrumbs*
*1 teaspoon cinnamon*
*1 teaspoon ginger*
*½ teaspoon salt*
*½ teaspoon baking soda*

*110g (4oz) butter*
*50g (2oz) caster sugar*
*110g (4oz) mixed fruit*
*1 tablespoon syrup*
*1 tablespoon treacle*
*1 egg*
*Milk to mix*

Mix the dry ingredients in the left-hand column. Rub in the butter and then add the sugar and mixed fruit. Warm the syrup and treacle and add with the beaten egg. Mix to a fairly thick consistency, adding a little milk if necessary. Steam in a covered bowl for three hours. Serve with a hot sweet white sauce.

## Pecan Pie – Angela Field

A Southern Baptist missionary gave me this traditional recipe from the state of Georgia, where pecans grow in profusion. You can substitute golden syrup if you cannot find corn syrup, which is slightly less sweet. Happy eating!

*1 cup white corn syrup*
*1 cup dark brown sugar*
*1/3 teaspoon salt*
*1/3 cup melted butter or margarine*
*1 teaspoon vanilla essence*

Combine all the above and then add:

*3 whole eggs, slightly beaten*

Pour mixture into a 23cm (9") unbaked shortcrust pastry case. Sprinkle over or arrange in concentric circles:

*1 heaped cup of whole shelled pecans*

Bake for forty-five minutes at 180C (350F, gas mark 4) and serve with cream or vanilla ice cream.

## Phillipa's Cheesecake – Phillipa Holloway

The clean natural taste of this cheesecake is perfect on its own, or it can be topped with fruit or plain chocolate, melted with a little butter.

Base:
*225g (8oz) digestive biscuits*
*110g (4oz) melted butter*

Crush biscuits finely (stamp on them in a strong plastic bag), add enough melted butter to bind and press into a deep push-up bottom tin. Chill.

Filling:
*700g (1½ lb) Philadelphia cheese, or Philly cheese and creme fraîche.*
*2 eggs*
*½ teaspoon real vanilla essence*
*225g (8oz) sugar*
*Pinch of salt*

Cream the cheese and sugar; add eggs one at a time (beating between each one); add vanilla. Beat well. Pour the mixture over the crumb case, bake in a slow oven 140C-150C (275-300F, gas mark 1-2) for 30 minutes. Switch off heat and leave in oven till cool. Chill for at least 2 hours or overnight.

## Mrs Marshallsay's Rice Pudding Story

As a young bride I accompanied my new husband when he applied for a job as a gardener on a millionaire's estate. I was asked if I would consider doing the weekend cooking. As the family had a house in London and did all their entertaining there, they said they only required very plain cooking at the weekend. And this was very easy, only the best ingredients, Steak and Kidney Pie made with Rump Steak and Lamb's Kidneys, etc. etc. and a super kitchen to work in. I was asked to make a Rice Pudding. All milk, not half milk, half water as my mum made it, and gold top milk at that, dotted with butter not marge, and served with cream and strawberry jam. I cooked it very slowly in their large American oven, watching as the top turned a gorgeous golden colour, and carefully took it out of the oven.

But I had forgotten to put the rice in!

## Promise Pudding – Elizabeth Megahey

Everyone loves this luscious pudding, which is a wonderful treat for those who must eat gluten-or wheat-free. The top is crunchy toasted almonds, underneath that is a lemony custard and at the bottom lies a fluffy apple purée. If you use a glass dish to bake it in, everyone can see the layers.

*675-775g (1½ -1¾ lbs) cooking apples*
*Grated rind and juice of a lemon*
*50g (2oz) golden caster sugar*
*4 large free-range eggs, separated*
*3 tablespoons runny honey*
*150ml (¼ pint) milk*
*25g (1oz) cornflour*
*Pinch cream of tartar*
*25g (1oz) flaked almonds*
*Pinch of salt*

Peel and core the apples. Cut them up coarsely and put them in a saucepan with a sprinkle of lemon juice (save most of the juice for later) and the sugar. Cover and cook over gentle heat stirring occasionally, until the apples are soft and fluffy. Pour into a 1.8 litre (3 pint) ovenproof glass dish and leave to cool.

To make the custard, put the yolks of the eggs in a bowl with the honey and whisk well. Beat in the remaining lemon juice, followed by the milk a little at a time. Add the cornflour and whisk until free of lumps. Add the grated lemon rind.

Heat the oven to 180C (350F, gas mark 4). Whisk the egg whites with the cream of tartar and salt until they stand up in soft peaks and then gently fold them into the lemon custard. Pour the mixture over the apple purée and sprinkle with the flaked almonds. Bake in the centre of the oven for about thirty minutes, until golden brown. Serve hot, with lashings of lovely wicked cream.

## Sally Lee's Tips

**Pears:** Stew in lemonade as a change from water.

## Proper Trifle – Tidal Favourites

The genuine article bears absolutely no resemblance to the stale bought cake soaked in cheap sherry, with powder-made custard poured over it, (we used to call it slime, as children) that often gives Trifle a bad name. This is a labour of love, to be proffered, not on the smartest of occasions, but to friends and family at times, such as Easter, when several are gathered to celebrate.
Start with the sponge, which has no raising agent except the air beaten into the eggs.

## Real Sponge Cake

Separate:
*5 eggs (free-range if possible)*
Beat the whites until foamy and slowly add:
*¼ cup (50g, 2oz) caster sugar*
In another bowl, beat yolks with:
*Juice of ½ a lemon*
When thick, gradually beat in:
*¾ cup (150g, 5oz) caster sugar*
Gently fold the whites into the yolks. Sift together and fold in:
*1 cup (150g, 5oz) plain white flour*
*¼ teaspoon salt*
Pour into three unbuttered shallow cake tins (preferably with rotating sliders to release cakes) or one large springform tin. Bake at 180C, 350F for 10 to 20 minutes, or until it bounces back from a quick finger prod. While the sponge is baking, make the custard.

## Real Custard

Put into a heavy (non stick) saucepan:
*6 (free-range) eggs,*
*1 cup (230g, 8oz) caster sugar*
*3 teaspoons real vanilla essence*
*1 ½ pints (850ml, 30fl oz) cream (double, single, top-off the milk, or any mixture of them)*
Whisk all together. Now you need patience. Stirring firmly (a flat-bottomed slotted wooden implement is best for this) right across the bottom of the whole pan, slowly bring the custard to blood heat. Test this with your finger; when it is too hot to bear you are nearly there. Continue to stir until the custard thinly coats the back of a silver spoon. By now your sponge(s) should be out of the oven and cooling on a wire rack. (A roving assistant is a help, here, or the acquisition of the six or so hands that all busy people seem to develop). Keep giving the custard a stir while it cools, to prevent a skin forming. Put the sponge into a large dish, big enough to contain it and all the custard. Soak it with sherry, Madeira or other sweet and suitable booze, spread (or dot) with good jam (home-made if you can get it, or make it), and pour the custard over it.

Traditionally, it is served covered with whipped cream and studded with slivered almonds, but this could be lily gilding. Good chocolate mini Easter eggs are a suitable decoration for it at the appropriate time; beware cheap seasonal trimmings, however, as their artificial flavours and colours can seep and run, spoiling both taste and appearance. Once people have tried Proper Trifle they nearly always come back for more; apart from taking a little time, it is not difficult to make. The only problem lies in stopping oneself and everyone else from scoffing the custard before it is poured over the sponge…

## Raspberry Mousse – Valentine Simson

*225g (8oz) raspberries*
*50g (2oz) caster sugar*
*220g (8fl oz) double cream*
*1 tablespoon Sherry*

Keep eight raspberries out for decoration and then place all the ingredients into a liquidiser and blend well. Pour into a serving bowl and chill. Decorate with the eight reserved raspberries and serve with sweet biscuits.

## Sultana Steamed Pudding – Linda Brewer

*110g (4oz) butter*
*110g (4oz) sugar*
*2 eggs*
*225g (8oz) self raising flour, sifted with*
*Pinch of salt*
*150ml (5fl oz) milk*
*3 tablespoons jam*
*175g (6oz) sultanas*

Cream the butter and the sugar together until fluffy. Beat in the eggs, then fold in the flour and salt alternately with the milk. Add the sultanas and fold into the mixture. Grease a 570ml (1-pint) microwavable pudding basin and place the jam on the bottom. Spoon the mixture on the top and cover. Place in the microwave for four to six minutes until well risen. Invert basin and serve pudding with hot custard.

## Tiramisu – Janet Gibbs

This is a delicious pudding for a dinner party or any special occasion. The recipe was given to me by a French chef whilst on holiday in Guernsey, so has wonderful memories for me of that island. Serves 4 – 6.

*Small chocolate sponge*
*4 eggs*
*225g (8oz) caster sugar*
*500g (1tub) Mascapone cheese*
*Small glass of Tia Maria, sherry and coffee mixed*

Beat together 4 egg yolks with half the caster sugar. Add tub of Mascapone to beaten egg yolks and sugar mix; set aside. Beat together 4 egg whites with the remaining sugar to make meringue mix. Fold into egg/Mascapone mixture.

Cut the chocolate sponge into thin slices and place in the bottom of individual glasses. Dribble the Tia Maria/Sherry/coffee mixture over the sponge. Cover with Mascapone mixture. Repeat process with the last layer being the egg, cheese and sugar mixture. Garnish with chocolate shavings or sprinkle with cocoa.

## Strawberry Ice Cream Squares – Jules Monier-Williams

An unusual way to use strawberries, this is delicious for summer supper parties.

*110g (4oz) flour*
*2 tablespoons brown sugar*
*50g (2oz) chopped walnuts*
*50g (2oz) melted butter*
*2 egg whites*
*225 (8oz) granulated sugar*
*570ml (1 pint) measure of sliced strawberries or raspberries*
*2 tablespoons lemon juice*
*275ml (½ pint) double cream*

Stir the first four ingredients together and spread into a shallow baking tin. Bake for twenty minutes at 180C (350F), forking occasionally. Sprinkle half the mixture into a freezer container. Combine egg whites, granulated sugar, strawberries and lemon juice in a bowl. Beat at high speed for ten minutes, and then cover with a damp cloth. Fold in whipped cream. Spoon this over the nut mixture in the freezer container. Spread the rest of the nut mixture on top and freeze. Remove from freezer half-to-one hour before serving and cut into squares.

## Strawberry Mousse – Tidal Favourites

Equally good made with raspberries and extra delicious topped with crunchy praline. It is light and fresh and a good mixer at parties when people want to try all the puds…

*450g (1lb) strawberries*
*230g (8oz) caster sugar*
*Juice and grated rind 1 lemon*
*1 packet gelatine with water to melt*
*250g (1carton) double cream*

Set the gelatine to melt with a little water in a basin over simmering water. Chobble the strawberries (or any other berries) in the blender, with half the sugar and the lemon juice and grated rind. Soft-whip the cream with the other half of the sugar and fold in the liquidised berries. Stir in the melted gelatine mix, pour into a pretty bowl and put in the fridge to set. Just before serving add the praline, (page 142) if you like the crunch; or decorate with a few reserved berries.

## Upside-down Pud – Tidal Favourites

My family likes this pud to have oodles of fruity goo underneath the cake-like topping. It is quick and easy to make, especially if you have American measuring cups and spoons.

Melt, in an ovenproof baking dish:

*½ cup (½ packet, 125g, 4½ oz) butter*
*1 cup (200g, 7oz) dark brown sugar*

Add *any fruit and juice you like, with accompanying spices. Tinned pineapples, pears, peaches or apricots are all good, as are peeled, cored and sliced fresh pears, apples with orange slices, or anything else in your fruit bowl. Mincemeat is good at Christmas.*

Then make the cake batter. Sift together:

*1 ½ cups (225g, 8oz) plain white flour*
*½ cup (110g, 4oz) caster sugar*
*2 teaspoons baking powder*
*½ teaspoon salt*

Mix:

*1 egg, well beaten*
*½ cup (110ml, 4fl oz) milk*
*½ cup (125g, 4½ oz) melted butter*

Stir gently into the flour mixture. Pour over the fruit and caramel. Bake at 200C (400F) until brown and crusty (20-25 minutes). Serve warm with pouring cream, vanilla ice cream, or **Fruit Sauce**. You can make this by creaming *a little tinned fruit juice* with *a tablespoon of* cornflour, adding *the rest of the juice and some lemon juice* and stirring while bringing to the boil. If the juice is unsweetened you may need to add some sugar to taste.

## White Chocolate Brulée – Peggy Warboys

This is a wonderful dessert for chocolate lovers. The white chocolate mixture is rich and goes perfectly with the caramel chip topping. Serve in small portions – tiny coffee cups make ideal containers. Serves six.

*1 x 150g bar white chocolate*
*1 x 142ml carton soured cream*
*1 tablespoon rum*
*1 x 150ml carton double cream*
*50g (2oz) granulated sugar*

Break the chocolate into a mixing bowl and set over a saucepan of hot (not boiling) water until melted. Remove the bowl from heat. Stir in the soured cream and then the rum. In a separate bowl beat the double cream into soft peaks. Fold gently into the chocolate mixture. Spoon into six individual ramekin dishes (glasses or pretty coffee cups). Chill in the refrigerator for several hours or overnight. Two hours before serving measure the sugar into a dry saucepan. Set over moderate heat and stir – the sugar will form soft lumps, then turn to a golden caramel. When it's the right colour, draw off the heat and pour into a lightly oiled baking tray or dinner plate that is large enough for the caramel to set in a thin layer. As the syrup cools, it becomes brittle and a gentle tap will break it into pieces. Select the bigger nicely shaped bits and perch them on top of the chocolate mixture. Keep chilled until serving time.

If you do not wish to bother with the caramel topping then just serve it with a little grated dark chocolate on top.

## White Chocolate Mocha Sauce – Tidal Favourites

You can use this as an icing over cup cakes, chocolate cake, or choux pastry; or as a sauce over meringues, bananas and cream, or anything that likes a vanilla coffee flavour.

*1 bar good white chocolate, made with real vanilla. (Lindt is excellent)*
*1 heaped teaspoon coffee granules (de-caff or regular) melted with 1 dessertspoon boiling water*

Melt the chocolate in a bowl over boiling water and add the coffee mix. Stir well. It sets to a soft goo. I nearly always need to double or triple these quantities, but then I have a large and greedy family…

## After All These Luscious Puds – A Reminder of Hard Times…

## Humanised Baby Milk – Jilly Palmer

I found this recipe in my mother's book of "Receipts". It was my sister Heather's formula milk as a baby. It is a reminder to all hard-pressed young mothers that life was even more difficult in 1922!

Sufficient for 24 hours.
Set 1 ½ quarts of new milk at night in a bowl (about 10" across).
Take the top cream off in the morning (12 oz) skimming very slowly and carefully not to waste any. After all the cream is off make the quantity up to 30 oz by pouring in some of the remaining milk.
Mix 5 level tablespoons of sugar of milk with 2 oz of lime water. Mix all together in a jug. Put the jug in a pan of water and sterilise to 155 degrees, and remain in the water for 10 minutes.
Then add 20 oz of boiling water to the mixture. Stand the jug in cold water, covered with clean muslin.
This mixture for 24 hour feeds at 4 months. Vary according to age.

## Sally Lee's Tips

**Fruit Pies:** Seal the edges with egg white to prevent the juice spilling out.

# Salads and Vegetable Dishes

## Creamy Leek Croustade – Anne Smith

Having a vegetarian guest for a meal can cause some problems for non-veggies who strive to create an interesting dish, which can be enjoyed by all the family. This is my favourite vegetarian recipe, which, with its nutty, savoury base and creamy topping, is impressive enough for a dinner party. I use a food processor to prepare the ingredients for the base:

*175g (6oz) fresh wholemeal breadcrumbs*
*50g (2oz) butter or margarine*
*100g (4oz) grated tasty cheddar cheese*
*100g (4oz) chopped mixed nuts*
*½ teaspoon mixed herbs*
*1 crushed clove of garlic*

For the sauce:

*3 medium sized leeks*
*1 x 400g tin chopped tomatoes*
*25g (1oz) plain flour*
*284ml (½ pint) milk*
*Salt and pepper to taste*
*4 tablespoons fresh wholemeal breadcrumbs*

For the base, put the breadcrumbs in a basin and rub in the butter; then add the remaining ingredients. Press the mixture into a 28 x 18 x 2.5cm (11 x 7 x 1 inch) tin. Bake at 220C (425F, gas mark 7) for fifteen to twenty minutes, until golden brown. If you have a fan oven it will take less time, so keep an eye on it. Meanwhile, slice the leeks, melt the butter in a large saucepan and sauté the leeks until they are soft. Stir in the flour and slowly add the milk, stirring constantly; bring to the boil, then reduce heat to a simmer. Add the remaining ingredients (except the breadcrumbs) and simmer for a few minutes; check the seasoning. Spoon this mixture over the base, sprinkle with the breadcrumbs and heat through in the oven at 180C (350F, gas mark 4) for twenty minutes. Serve at once. This dish is particularly nice served with creamy mashed potatoes and green vegetables.

## Dressed Sprouts – Yvonne Adams

If sprouts are frowned on in your family, as in mine, this is an easy solution to avoid the cooking smell, especially if you are using this seasonal vegetable for guests.

Clean and slice your sprouts in half. Toss into boiling water and cook briefly just to soften. Drain, cool and toss in French dressing. They can be prepared well in advance of a meal and are most palatable.

## Exotic Salad – Yvonne Adams

Blow the price – have a treat!

*Baby sweet corn*
*Asparagus*
*Broccoli cut into small florets*
*Toasted flaked almonds (optional)*

Lightly cook baby sweet corn, asparagus and broccoli in salted water. Drain and cut into forkable lengths. Mix together with a salad dressing of your choice.

## Farmhouse Potatoes – Jilly Palmer

Fry chopped onions. Stir in roughly chopped cooked potatoes. Season.

## Potatoes Anna – Tidal Favourites

Anna is a good dinner party standby, as you can leave her happily baking in either a fast or slow oven until you need her.

*Potatoes*
*Onions, if wished*
*Olive oil*
*Garlic, if wished*
*Salt and pepper*

Use good large clean potatoes and slice them thinly with their skins on. Fry the chopped onions (if using) and layer, with the chopped garlic (if using) and the sliced potatoes into a baking dish with a little olive oil spread over the bottom. Salt and pepper the layers generously. Drizzle olive oil over the top, or dot with butter and bake for an hour in a high oven or two hours in a low oven. A good addition for a family supper, or as a main dish for veggies, is a generous layer of strong Cheddar over the top. Perhaps this version should be called Emily?

## Cheesy Baked Potatoes

Another good supper dish, and good for feeding veggies, is this rich and creamy, slightly curried filling for potatoes baked in their skins. Serves four

*Four large clean potatoes with good skins*
*1 x 150g packet of Boursin garlic and fines herbes cheese*
*75ml (3 fl oz) or so of milk (enough to make a slightly sloppy mixture)*
*2 teaspoons of mild curry powder (or more)*
*Salt and pepper*

Bake the potatoes. You can hurry them up by giving them ten minutes or so in the microwave and a half-hour burst in a hot oven to crisp them up. When crisp without and soft within, halve them and scoop the flesh into a saucepan in which you have already heated the other ingredients. Mash them until they are smooth and lovely and pile the mix back into the skins when you are happy with the seasonings. You can finish them with a shake of cayenne or paprika, or grated cheese. They can then be popped back in the oven until you are ready for them, or eaten immediately with, perhaps, a snipping of herbs over them.

## Fondue La Manche – Sam Chalmers

A lot of good things in life start with a C, and there is not a lot to beat a Cheese Fondue with Crudités, Claret and good Company. I only ever experienced cheese fondues made with white wine and Kirsch, until visiting friends in Holland, where we had one made with beer instead of wine. It was very good. So why not a Dorset/Normandy-style fondue with Cider and Calvados?

Melt, in a fondue pot on the stove:

*100g (3½ oz) butter*

Add, stirring all the time, of course, with a wooden spoon in a figure of eight:

*A little crushed garlic and lemon juice*
*250g (9 oz) flour*
*1 litre (1¾ pints) or so of cider, a little at a time*
*1kg (2lbs 3oz) any mature cheese*
*500g (just over 1lb) Emmentaler, Maaslander or equivalent cheese*
*Nutmeg, pepper, paprika, as desired*
*A little paste of cornflour and cider, to thicken, if you need to*

When the cheese has melted into a uniform mix and starts to bubble and just before transferring to the fondue stand, add:

*1 egg yolk*
*A splash of Calvados*

In addition to crusty bread, crudités of blanched cauliflower and broccoli florets, cherry tomatoes and cooked and cooled new potatoes may be served, or any other fondue-forkable vegetables that you may prefer. A good red Bordeaux completes the ensemble. Voilà Fondue La Manche!

## Ishtoo – Sam Chalmers

Coconut and lime trees grow in every garden in Kerala, the tropical, monsoon Malabar Coast of Southwest India. Ishtoo is a traditional potato-based vegetable dish, using coconut milk and lime juice.

*Peeled and cubed potatoes*
*Onions, a quarter the weight of the potatoes*
*Green chilli*
*Fresh ginger, peeled and sliced into matchsticks*
*Curry leaves*
*Salt*
*Coconut milk, fresh or tinned "cream of coconut"*
*Lime juice*

Boil peeled and cubed potatoes (with just enough water to cover) together with sliced onions, green chilli and thin sticks of fresh ginger. A few "curry leaves" (known as Vaypila in Kerala) should also be added, but these are unlikely to be found in England. Try using fresh bay leaves or chopped coriander leaves. After cooking, add salt and coconut milk and blend carefully with a wooden spoon, bringing once more to the boil. Turn off the heat and add the juice of a freshly squeezed, golf-ball-sized lime.

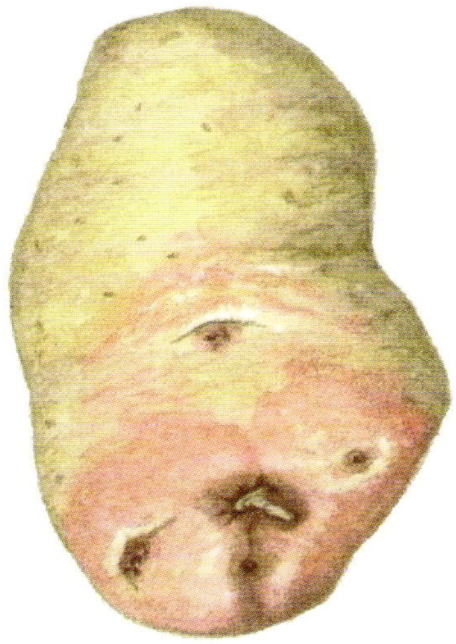

## Kartoffel Salat (Potato Salad) – Jilly Palmer

The Germans are wizards at cooking potatoes in many ways. This version of potato salad is delicious. Serve with cold meats.

*2 kilo potatoes*
*2 big spiced cucumbers (sweet pickled gherkins)*
*2 mild onions, chopped*
*½ cup mayonnaise*
*½ cup sour cream*
*Pepper, salt, wine vinegar, sugar to taste*

Cook the potatoes in their skins. Cool and peel and cut in slices. In another bowl combine all the other ingredients. Taste. Combine mixture carefully with the potatoes. Decorate with hard-boiled egg and tomato slices and parsley, as liked.

## Nut Loaf – Sally Lee

*450g (1 lb) coarse ground Brazil nuts (or mixed nuts)*
*450g (1 lb) tin tomatoes, liquidised*
*175g (6oz) breadcrumbs (I like wholemeal or granary)*
*2 teaspoons mixed herbs*
*1 tablespoon mild curry powder*
*2 eggs, lightly beaten*
*1 onion, chopped and gently sautéed until translucent*
*1 pepper, chopped and sautéed*

Mix all together and put into a lined loaf tin. Bake in oven at 170C (325F) for forty minutes. Eat warm or cold.

## Pepper Salad with Capers – Joan Naylor

An unusual and colourful salad, this is ideal for serving with fish dishes or light meals. If you are transporting it to a supper party, carry the dressing separately in a suitable closed container – or ingredients may be destined to liberally decorate the inside of one's car – as happened to me on one truly memorable occasion! Serves four to six.

*3 large peppers, red, green and yellow*
*90ml (6 tablespoons) olive oil*
*1 clove garlic, peeled and finely chopped*
*Fresh marjoram and basil, roughly chopped*
*30ml (2 tablespoons) capers*
*15ml (1 tablespoon) white wine vinegar*

Cut the peppers in half and remove the core and seeds. Press with the palm of the hand or the back of the knife to flatten. Brush the skin side with oil and place the peppers under a pre-heated grill. Grill the peppers until the skins are well charred. Wrap in a tea towel and leave for fifteen minutes. Unwrap and peel off the charred skin. Cut the peppers into thick strips and arrange on a serving dish. Scatter over the chopped garlic, basil leaves, marjoram and capers. Mix together the remaining olive oil with the vinegar, salt and pepper and pour over the salad. Refrigerate for one hour before serving.

## Quick Tuna Salad – Trish Rudd

Serves three to four.

*Small tin of tuna in brine, drained*
*Half a small iceberg lettuce, shredded*
*2 firm tomatoes, thinly sliced*
*About ¼ of a cucumber, thinly sliced*
*½ a green, red or yellow pepper, or a combination of all three, sliced*
*8 pitted black olives, halved*
*2 large spring onions, sliced*

Throw everything into a salad bowl; add salt, pepper, and a squeeze of lemon to taste. Toss generously. Easy, quick and very yummy.

## Red Salad – Yvonne Adams

*Red peppers, sliced*
*Red cabbage, finely shredded*
*Beetroot, sliced*
*Red onion, finely sliced*
*Radishes*
*Raspberry vinegar*
*Oil*
*Salt and pepper*

Make four downward cuts in a noughts and crosses pattern in the radishes and put them in water until they open up like water lilies. Put aside. Mix salad together with dressing. Put some beetroot slices on top with red onion rings around. Place water lily radishes as though floating on a raft of circular leaves. Red apple could be sliced in, too. It looks pleasant served next to a green salad.

## Sparkly Courgettes with Grated Cheese – Tidal Favourites

Courgettes are a good standby, if sometimes a little dull. This version can be sparkled up or down according to how much Tabasco you sprinkle over the layers. It would supply a vegetarian main course or a starter or side-vegetable for anyone.

Use quantities to suit.

*Courgettes, sliced*
*Salt and pepper*
*Worcester sauce, Tabasco*
*Strong cheddar, grated*
*Olive oil*

Pour a smidgen of oil into an ovenproof shallow dish and spread it thinly round to prevent sticking. Sprinkle the seasonings into the oil and turn the sliced courgettes in it, before layering them with the grated cheese, finishing with cheese on top. (Or sprinkle the Tabasco etc over the courgettes as you layer them, although you may get "hot spots" with this method.) Bake for about forty-five minutes in a medium oven; more or less time and heat according to circumstances. Full blast grill will speed things up.

## Two Vegan Recipes – Val Axtell

### Soya Cheese

*500g (1 lb 2oz) soya flour*
*500g (1 lb 2oz) margarine (Grandose sunflower)*
*340g (11oz) jar yeast extract*
*1 teaspoon chilli pepper or black pepper*

Slightly warm margarine and yeast extract. Beat all ingredients together in food mixer, put into plastic boxes, mark into squares and keep in fridge. Use as milk cheese either raw or cooked.

### Beetroot and Beans

*450g (1 lb) raw beetroot, peeled and chopped*
*1 tin red beans, drained*
*1 tin rich tomatoes*
*2 red peppers, chopped*
*1 red chilli, chopped*
*Garlic and onion to taste*

Cook beetroot in the microwave or on the hob with as little water as possible. Add all ingredients together and cook slowly for at least half an hour, or until it looks and smells done. Serve over pasta or rice with a sprinkle of soya cheese.

# Savoury Sauces, Dips and Relishes

**Marmande Tomatoes**

## Tomato Sauce for Bangers and Mash – Tidal Favourites

Cooked tomatoes are good for you – it's official! They contain lots of easy-to-get-at lycopenes, which are known anti-cancer agents, especially protective for the men in your life, but useful for all of us. It's a slimmers' sauce as well, as whatever theory of weight-loss regime one is currently adhering to, it has neither refined carbohydrates nor cream. The olive oil for softening the onions is full of the right kind of essential fatty acids, and protects the heart; onions boost the immune system; and, of course, garlic sends all demons running for cover. Still, never mind, as our friend Vulture would say: if it's delicious I'll eat it in spite of it's being healthy…

It freezes well, goes with all sorts of things, such as steak or fish or grilled chops, and keeps, cling-filmed, in the fridge for several days. Serves about eight people, depending on how sloppy they like their food. You can vary the quantities according to what's available and how much you like the ingredients.

*Olive oil, for frying*
*Two large onions, finely chopped*
*Two red peppers, finely chopped*
*A thumb's length of fresh ginger, peeled and chopped small*
*4 fat cloves of garlic, chopped*
*2 large or 4 medium tins of chopped tomatoes*
*A splodge of honey (optional, but it helps balance the acidity of the tomatoes)*
*Tamari soy sauce (if you can get it – no wheat – health food shops stock it)*
*Sea salt if not using soy sauce*
*Black pepper, Worcestershire sauce, Tabasco, paprika, chilli powder, to taste as liked*
*2 bay leaves or any other fresh herbs to hand.*

Start with the onions softened in olive oil over medium heat; add the peppers, ginger and garlic. When these have cooked, add all the other ingredients and simmer for ten minutes or so. Pep it up with hot spices if you like, especially to help clear a cold; or leave it cool, calm and collected. Serve hot or cold.

## Beetroot Chutney – Jill Harrison

With its lovely colour, this unusual chutney is good for Christmas presents, or, indeed, any time.

*900g (2lbs) beetroot*
*1 tablespoon salt*
*450g (1lb) apples*
*3 or 4 small onions*
*570ml (1 pint) vinegar*
*225g (½ lb) sugar*
*½ teaspoon ground ginger*
*Juice of 1 lemon*

Cook beetroot in salted water for one hour. When cold, peel and grate them, or cut into cubes. Peel apples and onions and chop them small. Simmer them with vinegar and sugar for twenty minutes. Add ginger and lemon juice and then the beetroot and simmer for a further twenty five minutes. Cool and pour into pots.

## Gingered Apple Sauce – Tidal Favourites

Wonderful with pork, gammon and lots of other meats, hot or cold, this version of an old favourite can be as hot and spicy – or not – as you like. Serves eight; or fewer and keeps for cold lunches…

*4 cooking apples*
*2 teaspoons (ad libitum) ground ginger*
*2 dessertspoons golden caster sugar*
*Juice of half a lemon*
*Salt and black pepper*
*Tabasco, as you like it*
*Cider, about half way up*

Peel, core and roughly chop the apples into a saucepan. Add the next five ingredients and then the cider, to about half way up the apples. Cook and stir occasionally until they have mushed nicely. Taste for seasoning and sparkle it up for more excitement if you like. I usually find that if it tastes just right without any other competing flavours then it will need more seasoning to be a piquant contrast to the rest of the food when on the plate… Serve hot or cold.

## Hollandaise Sauce – Tidal Favourites

This was the first grown-up cooking I learnt at my mother's knee, and I have used it all my life. It is wonderful with simply cooked fish and poured over broccoli, cauliflower and asparagus. It is simple, rich and foolproof.

*3 egg yolks, preferably free-range*
*Juice of 1 lemon*
*¾ of a 250g pack of slightly salted butter*

Put the whites, covered, in the fridge to make meringues with when you have a moment. Set the yolks and lemon juice in a bowl or *bain-marie* over simmering water. Cut the butter into three pieces and stir with a fork into the egg liaison, one piece at a time. When assimilated, remove from heat or it may curdle. It will keep hot for a few minutes, until you are ready to serve it.

## Mango Relish – Tidal Favourites

Something a little hot and spicy makes a good contrast to cold or plain-grilled meat. This really sparks up grilled duck breast, but it won't take the roof off your mouth… It's also very simple to make. You can easily double or quadruple the quantities for making Christmas prezzies.

*1 ripe mango, peeled and roughly chopped*
*1 lime, zest and juice*
*85g (3oz) golden caster sugar*
*2 tablespoons balsamic vinegar*
*25g (1oz) broken pecans or walnuts*
*1 teaspoon ground ginger*
*1 teaspoon turmeric*
*½ teaspoon cayenne pepper*
*¼ nutmeg, freshly grated*
*Salt and pepper*

Balsamic vinegar tastes the best, but darkens the relish. White wine vinegar will help it to keep its golden colour.

Boil all ingredients together for twenty minutes or so. Cool and pour into a clean jam jar.

## Minotaur Sauce – Tidal Favourites

In our part of the world we are fortunate enough to be able to buy superb, locally reared and naturally fed beef; therefore a roast wing rib features, by request, on festive days. Real **Horseradish Sauce** is a splendid accompaniment (see below) but on one occasion before our own root had taken hold in the garden, and we had no jars of plain, grated horseradish, I had to improvise. The result was approved and named by the friends in whose honour it was made. You can pep it up as much as you like; add even more garlic, Tabasco and ginger, though if your feast is on a Saturday night and you wish to attend church in the morning, you may feel constrained to sit in a back pew in a side aisle. The Minotaur was ever prone to bellow fire and brimstone.

You can put the ingredients straight into your sauceboat:

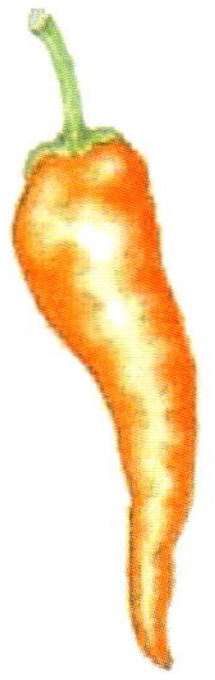

*Juice of half a lemon*
*1 dessertspoon honey or brown sugar*
*1 dessertspoon each of grainy mustard and Dijon mustard*
*1 finely chopped garlic clove or an inch or so of purée*
*1 dessertspoon fresh, peeled and grated or finely chopped ginger*
*Several dashes of Tabasco, to taste*
*Pinch of sea salt, several grinds of black pepper*
*1 carton (284ml, 10fl oz) double cream*

Combine all by stirring with a fork; it thickens immediately. Refrigerate until serving. This sauce goes well with several hot or cold meats besides beef, especially ham or gammon.

## Horseradish Sauce

Quantities are variable according to what you have to hand; as long as you have access to plain, grated horseradish, fresh or bottled, it's almost as quick to fling these ingredients together as to open a jar. Beware if you grate your own: it will make your eyes water if you peer too closely into the blender! Your diners will be surprised, for although this should have bite, it is nothing like as sharp as most commercial varieties.

*1 horseradish root, peeled and chobbled fine in the blender, or*
*1 jar plain grated horseradish*
*Juice of half a lemon*
*1 teaspoon sugar*
*A little chopped garlic or garlic purée (optional)*
*1 carton cream or crème fraîche*
*Salt and pepper*

Stir all together and taste to see if you'd like a little more of this or that.

## Red Onion Marmalade - Kevin Booker

The sweet/sour tang of this "marmalade" is good with Bacon Floddie and with all sorts of meats.

*1 red onion*
*Olive oil for frying*
*Juice of an orange*
*1 tablespoon maple syrup*
*1 tablespoon balsamic vinegar*
*Salt and pepper*

Slice the onion thinly and put in a saucepan with a drop of olive oil. Cook until soft. Add the orange juice, syrup and vinegar. Cook over high heat until all the liquid has gone. Season and serve warm.

## Seriously Hot Sauce – Trish Rudd

As a contrast to mild and creamy dips, served with crunchy raw vegetables or crisps as a party starter, this can be a real shocker. Curiously enough though, after the first surprised reaction, people nearly always come back for more.

*1 large onion chopped*
*2 crushed cloves of garlic*
*3-4 large tomatoes, chopped (red or green)*
*205ml (7 fl oz) water*
*1 teaspoon salt*
*1 teaspoon cumin*
*¼ teaspoon ground coriander*
*2 teaspoon red wine*
*½ teaspoon black pepper*
*½ teaspoon chilli paste/powder*
*2 tablespoons tomato paste/puree*
*2 tablespoons olive oil*
*Cayenne pepper, shaken in, to taste*

Sauté onions and garlic in the olive oil in a saucepan with ½ tsp. salt until the onions are clear. Add the spices, then the tomatoes, water, pastes, remaining salt and wine. Cover and simmer for at least ½ an hour, the longer the better. Add cayenne pepper a little at a time. The longer the sauce cooks the hotter it is likely to get, so beware.

## Tarragon Mayonnaise – Caroline Norman

A green, fresh-tasting mayonnaise seems to be especially popular with summer dishes like poached salmon.

*1 large free-range egg*
*1 teaspoon dry mustard*
*1 tablespoon vinegar*
*A good handful of fresh snipped tarragon or dill*
*1 heaped teaspoon sugar*
*Olive oil*

Put every thing except the oil in the blender and chobble. Pour in the oil until thick.

## Tuna Fish Dip – Valentine Simson

*1 tin tuna, drained*
*225g (8oz) cream cheese*
*1 teaspoon curry powder*
*Salt and pepper*

Put all the ingredients in a blender and mix until well blended. Turn into ramekin dishes and cover with clingfilm. Chill. When ready to serve, place ramekins onto large plates, surround with tortilla chips and eat – delicious!

## Uncle Bill's Salad Dressing – Jilly Palmer

We never met Uncle Bill, but frequently enjoyed his salad dressing.

*3 tablespoons caster sugar*
*4 tablespoons tomato ketchup*
*3 tablespoons wine vinegar*
*1 tablespoon balsamic vinegar*
*1 cup vegetable or olive oil, or half-and-half*
*Salt and freshly ground black pepper*
*1 small onion, chopped*

Mix all ingredients except oil in a jam jar or liquidiser. Add oil gradually.

## Simple Mayonnaise – Tidal Favourites

*4 egg yolks*
*1 teaspoon sugar*
*1 dessertspoon mustard, any kind you like*
*2 tablespoons white wine vinegar*
*Salt and pepper*
*Oil (olive, sunflower or a mixture)*

Whizz the first five ingredients in the blender. Slowly pour in the oil until thick. Taste for seasoning. You may like more vinegar, or perhaps lemon juice.

# Soups

Nettle, Buddleia and Butterflies

## Apple and Stilton Soup – Josie Pleavin

Serves four to six.

*450g (1 lb) eating apples (Cox or Ellison, etc.)*
*30g (1oz) butter*
*1 tablespoon sunflower oil*
*225g (8oz) onion, finely diced*
*225g (8oz) potatoes, finely diced*
*1.2 litres (2 pints) vegetable or chicken stock*
*115g (4oz) blue Stilton*
*Salt and freshly ground black pepper*

Core but do not peel the apples and cut into walnut sized pieces. Heat the butter and oil in a pan and add onions and potatoes. Fry over a medium heat for three to four minutes until onions have softened. Season generously. Pour in the stock and add apple pieces. Bring to boil and simmer for fifteen minutes until fruit and vegetables are soft. Liquidize. Add 60g (2 oz) of the Stilton and liquidize again. Crumble remaining Stilton with a fork. Ladle soup into warm bowls and top with the crumbled Stilton.

## Artichoke Soup – Anne Dickson

*700 g (1½ lb) Jerusalem artichokes*
*Juice of 1 lemon*
*1 onion*
*½ cucumber*
*275ml (½ pint) double cream*
*50g (2oz) butter*
*845ml (1½ pints) chicken stock*
*Parsley stalks*
*Salt and pepper*

Peel and cut artichokes into ½ inch chunks and leave in cold water with the lemon juice. Peel and slice onion, wipe and slice cucumber. Drain and dry artichokes in cloth. Cook in butter with onions and cucumber for five minutes over low heat. Do not brown. Pour over stock; add parsley stalks, salt and pepper. Bring to boil and simmer for about twenty minutes or until vegetables are soft. Remove from heat and after cooling slightly put in liquidiser. Blend until smooth, adjust seasoning and stir in cream. Bring to simmering point just before serving.

## Cullen Skink – Mary Coles

*Onions*
*Potatoes*
*Smoked haddock*
*Milk – ½ pan*
*Seasoning*

Quantities vary according to numbers catered for. Chop the onion, cook but do not brown. Flake the fish. Boil the potatoes; dice or slice into the milk. Add the fish and onion. **Do not let the milk boil.** The soup should come out thick, but not too thick. Finish off with a little cream if required.

## Avgolemono – Geoffrey Donald

This is a traditional Greek lemon soup, garnished with cream and set white of egg. It can be served either hot or cold.

For about four helpings:

*One medium lemon*
*A good knob of butter*
*Either 3 shallots or a bunch of spring onions*
*A heaped tablespoon cornflour*
*1.2 litres (2 pints) chicken stock*
*3 eggs*
*4 tablespoons double cream, lightly whipped*
*3 or 4 tablespoons single cream*
*Salt and black pepper*

Finely chop the shallots, or top and tail the spring onions, cutting them into half-inch lengths (include some of the green stem too). Melt the butter in a pan and sauté them until they just begin to colour but not brown. Remove from the heat and stir in the flour until it amalgamates with the hot butter. Add the stock all at once, stirring vigorously to blend in the flour. Bring to the boil and simmer gently for ten minutes. Meanwhile, wash the lemon and extract the zest from the surface of the peel, either by rubbing it on a fine grater over a plate, or by carefully paring off just the thin yellow outside. Add this to the pan, together with the juice. Simmer for a further five minutes or so. Now strain the liquid, discard the solids, rinse out the pan and return the liquid to it. It can be reserved until the next day if necessary.

Separate the egg whites from their yolks. Beat the whites with a fork just sufficiently to loosen the texture; blend in the single cream, and season with a little salt and pepper. Pour into a shallow dish such as the top of a Pyrex ovenware bowl and bake in the oven at about 180C (350F) until just solid. Set aside and allow to cool.

If necessary, reheat the soup and stir a little into the egg yolks before adding them to the pan, stirring the while. Bring back to a simmer but do not boil. Now is the time to cool and chill in the refrigerator if it is to be served cold. If hot, then serve directly into the bowls. For the final garnish, divide the cooked egg white into a portion for each, and add it with a tablespoon of the whipped double cream.

## Avocado or Cucumber Soup – Tidal Favourites

My daughter requested this soup for a birthday dinner party, having met it elsewhere; she wondered whether she should find the recipe for me. I thought we could probably manage with this variation of an avocado dip that was an old favourite, and the result was a most gratifying success. It is a very pretty pale green. For cucumber soup, simply substitute cucumber for avocado and proceed the same way. Quantities are per person.

*½ an avocado (or ½ a cucumber)*
*150ml (5fl oz or ¼ pint) milk*
*A generous squeeze of lemon juice*
*1 tablespoon cream*
*1 sliced spring onion or snipping of chives*
*Sea salt, black pepper, Worcester sauce, Tabasco, to taste*

Put the peeled stoned avocado into the blender with all the other ingredients. If you are making for eight people or so you may need to work with half at a time. Chobble away until the mixture is completely smooth. Taste and adjust seasonings; you will need plenty of black pepper. If it tastes flat, add a little more lemon juice and perhaps salt. You can substitute *crème fraîche* or *yogurt* for the cream if you like a sharper version. The soup should be quite thick and creamy, but slurpable.

Pour it into a serving jug and cover with cling film touching the soup to prevent it browning. Chill until serving time. Freshly chopped herbs such as *chives, parsley or tarragon* are good, sprinkled into each bowl as you serve it.

Note: to make the dip from which this originated, simply leave out the milk and step up the Tabasco.

## Bloody Mary Soup – Jilly Palmer

Marvellous, and especially if you have an oft-travelling son who brings you a whopping big bottle of duty-free Vodka!

*2 tablespoons butter*
*1 finely chopped onion*
*3 diced sticks of celery*
*2 tablespoons tomato purée*
*1 tablespoon sugar*
*5 cups tomato juice*
*2 teaspoons Worcestershire Sauce*
*Salt and ground pepper to taste*
*Dash lemon juice*
*4 tablespoons Vodka – or let your hand slip slightly…*

Melt butter and gently fry the onions and celery. Stir in the tomato purée and sugar; add the tomato juice and simmer for ten minutes. Add the remaining ingredients. Liquidise. Serve hot or chilled. A blob of sour cream and a little "caviar" makes it an exotic starter.

## Cream of Spinach and Coconut Soup – Anne Watts

Given to me by a friend, this recipe seems to be an unusual combination of flavours – but it tastes delicious... Serves four.

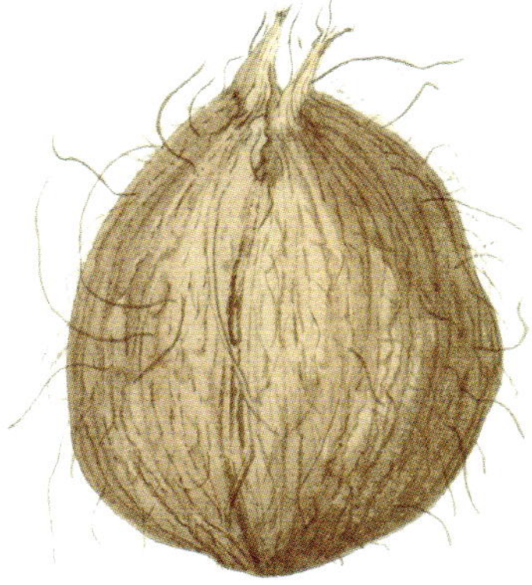

*25g (1oz) butter or margarine*
*1 onion, chopped*
*1 potato, chopped*
*450g (1 lb) spinach, chopped*
*750ml (1¼ pints) vegetable stock*
*50g (2oz) creamed coconut*
*150ml (¼ pint) single cream or milk*
*Seasoning*

Heat butter in a large pan. Add onion and potato and cook gently for five minutes, stirring occasionally to prevent sticking. Add chopped spinach and stock. Cover and simmer gently for fifteen minutes or until the vegetables are tender. Do not overcook or the spinach will lose its bright green colour. Add coconut and purée in a blender. Return mixture to the pan and stir in cream or milk. Season to taste and reheat carefully.

## Curried Parsnip Soup – Jules Monier-Williams

A wonderful winter warmer! Serves four to six.

*450g (1 lb) parsnips*
*1 onion, chopped*
*50g (2oz) butter*
*1 tablespoon mild curry paste or powder*
*15g (½ oz) flour*
*1 litre (1¾ pint) chicken stock*
*1 tablespoon parsley, chopped*
*Pinch of thyme*
*Salt and pepper*
*2 tablespoons crème fraîche*

Melt butter in a saucepan and sauté the parsnips and onion until soft. Stir in curry paste or powder and blend well. Add stock, herbs, salt and pepper to taste. Simmer for thirty minutes, stirring occasionally. Blend until smooth in a liquidizer. Add the crème fraîche and blend again. Heat through and check seasonings before serving.

## Garlic Soup with Poached Egg – Geoffrey Donald

This is one variant of a Spanish recipe characteristic of the Castille region, where it can be found as 'Sopa Castellana'. Sometimes finely chopped vegetables or tiny cubes of ham are added. One can experiment... Its main characteristic is to be served boiling in very hot glazed earthenware bowls so that a whole egg, added at the last minute, poaches on the way to the table. If it is not boiling hot, the egg stays glutinous and horrid!
Serves four.

*2 or 3 rashers of lean bacon*
*Olive oil to fry and sauté*
*Five or six cloves of garlic, sliced large enough to find later*
*1.2litres (2 pints) or so of water*
*½ an onion, finely chopped*
*Tablespoon chopped parsley*
*Bouquet garni*
*Salt and black pepper*
*Paprika to colour*
*Four eggs, broken into individual cups*

Chop the bacon into inch squares and fry in a little of the oil until nicely crisp. Remove and keep for later. Add more oil to the frying pan and sauté the chopped onion, parsley and garlic together until the onion is just coloured but not dark brown. Fish out the garlic, which should be easy to spot as being lighter coloured and garlic-like... Scrape all the remainder into a casserole pan. Add the water, salt and pepper and the bouquet garni. Bring to the boil and simmer gently for say half an hour to let the flavours move into the liquid. Towards the end, sprinkle a little paprika in to colour it. At this stage it could be left to cool for serving the next day. Have ready very hot soup bowls (preferably ovenproof). Bring the soup to the boil. Quickly ladle a serving into a bowl; immediately add the egg while the liquid is still moving, otherwise it will sink to the bottom and not poach. Add a portion of the bacon, and serve rapidly. Note: traditionally, in Spain, this is served with a slice of crisply toasted bread in the soup.

## Mushroom Soup with Madeira – Josie Pleavin

Serves four.

*75g (3oz) butter*
*1 large onion*
*500g (1 lb) mushrooms, finely chopped*
*25g (1oz) plain flour*
*900ml (1½ pints) chicken stock*
*Salt and pepper*
*120ml (4 fl oz) dry Madeira*
*150 ml (¼ pint) double cream*
*Chopped parsley to garnish*

Melt butter in a large pan, add onion and cook for 20 minutes or until evenly browned. Add the mushrooms and cook for 2 minutes. Stir in flour and cook for 1 minute. Gradually stir in the stock and season with salt and pepper to taste. Bring to the boil, cover and simmer for 10 minutes. Stir in the Madeira and cream and heat through gently. Serve immediately, garnished with parsley.

## Peanut Butter Soup – Trish Rudd

This was a favourite of ours as children in Ghana, where my brothers, sister and I spent the early part of our childhood. My mother adapted it, when we came to live in England, to use the ingredients that were available in the sixties.

*1 large jar peanut butter*
*2 chicken breasts, skinned and cubed*
*A little flour, seasoned*
*1 large onion, chopped*
*3-4 large tomatoes, peeled and chopped*
*570ml (1pint) or so of chicken stock*
*Garlic, crushed or chopped, as much or as little as you like*
*Chilli, chopped fresh or powdered, as much as you like*
*Salt and pepper*
*A little oil*

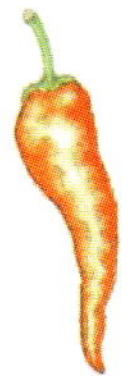

Roll the chicken pieces in the seasoned flour and brown in a little oil. Add onions and garlic and stir. Cook until the onions are softened and add the tomatoes and chilli. Cook for a few minutes and then slowly add the stock, stirring continuously. Cook for about fifteen to twenty minutes. Pour the peanut butter into a bowl; add some of the stock from the soup and mix together until it is possible to pour it into the saucepan. Cook gently for a further fifteen to twenty minutes or until the chicken is tender. If you feel really adventurous you can add some okra to it, in which case it's best to cook it first and then add it. You can also thicken the soup with a roux and eat the "stew" with African yams.

## Vegetable Soup to Keep You Slim – Jilly Palmer

This soup is full of good things, none of them fattening. It can be livened up with a dash of chilli sherry, or made delicious, but not so slender-making, with a sprinkling of grated cheese. It serves about six or seven people at once, or one or two slimmers over a period of days, if kept in the fridge.

*6 large onions and/or leeks*
*1 head celery*
*1 cabbage*
*225g (½ lb) mushrooms*
*2 peppers, red, green or yellow*
*350g (12oz) tin tomatoes*
*1 jar tomato Ragu*
*4 chicken stock cubes made up with 2.25litres (4 pints) boiling water (or your own stock)*

Cut vegetables into large chunks and put in a large pan with tomatoes and stock. Boil for ten minutes, and then simmer. Season with salt, pepper, parsley or even curry powder and spices.

## Stinging Nettle Soup – Wendy Turney

While on your rambles you can be preparing your supper. Pick:

*A large pan of nettle tips (use only young new ones, not old stalks)*

Wash them well and cook in a small amount of water – lid off so the sting evaporates!
Make about

*570ml (1 pint) thick white sauce*

When the nettles are cooked sufficiently (that is – purée by stirring) remove from heat, add:

*A knob of butter*
*1 onion, finely chopped*

Cook for a further five minutes. Mix altogether. Add *milk* to taste. Good luck!
Note: Nettles are good food for butterflies (or their caterpillars), too…

## Three Root Soup – Chris Eldred

Blended root vegetables can form the base of smooth and creamy soups, which need no added flour, cream or egg yolks. In this one, half the vegetables are puréed and the other half left in pieces to give an interesting texture.

*225g (½ lb) swede*
*225g (½ lb) parsnips*
*225g (½ lb) carrots*
*1 medium onion, chopped*
*25g (1oz) butter*
*845 ml (1½ pints) vegetable stock*
*1 bouquet garni*
*Sea salt and freshly ground black pepper*
*1 tablespoon fresh chopped parsley*
*1 tablespoon fresh chopped chervil*

Sauté the onion in the butter until brown. Meanwhile, cut the root vegetables into large chunks. Add them to the onions and sweat for five minutes. Add the stock, salt and pepper and the bouquet garni and bring to the boil.

Cover and simmer for twenty-five minutes on very low heat. Add the other herbs and cook for a further ten minutes. Blend half the soup in a liquidizer or blender, return to the pan, mix and serve immediately, with crusty poppy seed rolls. Wonderful!

## The Return of the Stock Pot – Tidal Favourites

My mother always kept a stockpot on the go, and her soups were wonderful. It is not a complicated procedure, even if you do work all the hours of the day and half the night. It simply means bunging the chicken carcass into a deep pot after you've devoured your roast, with half an onion, the leftover gravy, any empty lemon halves to hand, the vegetable water (but not brassicas) salt, pepper, a bay leaf, and boiling it up merrily every day. If you forget to boil it, and it starts gently to heave of its own accord, throw it on the compost heap, which will love it. You can keep adding things to it, during its daily boil, except for any cabbagey things, which would remind you of school dining rooms when you were late for lunch. Don't add lamb, either, unless you're making a purely lamb broth, and the same applies to fish. Otherwise, almost anything goes, and it will be the basis for soups and gravies that you know are gluten free, which most commercially prepared ones are not.

This soup, and your basic stock, can easily be frozen (I use plastic ice cream boxes) and hauled out any time you don't have your stockpot bubbling away. In fact it's a good idea to do this, as you may not have a boiling ring always to spare for the famous pot. Turkey makes a particularly good stock, as does pheasant. Goose and duck are a bit fatty, though you can always cool the liquor in the fridge and skim it before freezing. Pure beef stock, made with shin and marrowbone, onion and carrot, is superb.

Now you can make:

## Pedal Bin Soup

*One large onion, chopped finely*
*Olive oil*
*Any leftover veg that hasn't grown whiskers in the fridge (not brassicas)*
*Garlic, if you like*
*Liquid from your stockpot, along with dregs from last night's wine, or more, lemon juice, and any thing else lurking which you want to use up, such as the remains of the coffee cream.*
*Cornflour*

Cook the onion (and garlic) in the oil until it smells delicious; take up the oil with corn flour or other plain flour, to make a loose roux. Add the cold liquids all at once, and stir like crazy over heat until the soup thickens and is smooth and glossy. Add your finely chopped veg and odds and ends, salt, pepper, any herbs and spices if it needs pepping up. At this stage, you can chobble it in the blender for a smoother soup, but it's more to wash up, and most people like wondering what all the bits are. Serve hot, perhaps with **Cheese Muffins**, lettuce, tomatoes and cheese on the side and there's lunch.

# Trisha Goddard's Travellers' Soup – Tidal Favourites

When we took a week's recuperative holiday in Spain, we stayed in a Wolsey Lodge house on the beach at Mijas called Casa Aloha: a most unusual and beautifully sited house, owned by Trisha and Ray Goddard. This was the nectar she served as a starter on our first night. Anything more reviving and refreshing for tired travellers would be hard to imagine. Serves six to eight.

*4 large red sweet peppers, seeded and roughly chopped*
*2 large leeks (white part only)*
*110g (4oz) butter*
*2 teaspoons ground ginger*
*2 heaped teaspoons sweet paprika*
*2 tablespoons caster sugar*
*1 teaspoon salt*
*Ground pepper to taste*
*Zest and juice of 1 large orange*
*570 ml (1 pint) chicken stock*
*570 ml (1 pint) plain yogurt*

Melt butter, without burning, and soften the chopped leeks and peppers with lid on, stirring from time to time. Add all seasonings and stock. Simmer for thirty minutes. Blend to a fine purée. Chill. Stir in yogurt. Chill again. Serve with toasted slivered almonds.

## Vegetarian Minestrone – Joan Naylor

A "come again" soup, this is delicious for lunch with crusty bread. Problem - finding a saucepan large enough to hold double the ingredients – just in case! There is always scope for adding whatever other ingredients one may be tempted to add – within reason! Serves eight.

*225 (8oz) dried white cannellini beans*
*30ml (2 tablespoons) olive oil*
*1 onion, chopped*
*2 cloves garlic, crushed*
*4 sticks celery, sliced*
*2 carrots, diced*
*120g (4oz) french beans, cut into 1-inch lengths*
*225g (8oz) peeled and diced (or use tinned tomatoes)*
*1 dried red chilli pepper*
*2.5 litres (5 pints) vegetarian stock*
*Salt and pepper*
*1 sprig fresh rosemary*
*1 bay leaf*
*3 potatoes, peeled and diced into small cubes*
*3 courgettes, trimmed and diced into small cubes*
*15ml (1 tablespoon) chopped fresh basil*
*15ml (1 tablespoon) chopped fresh parsley*

Place the beans in a large bowl, cover with cold water and leave to soak overnight. Heat the oil in a large stockpot and add onion and garlic. Cook until onion has softened but not coloured. Add the celery, carrots and green beans. Drain the cannellini beans and add them to the pot with the tomatoes and the chilli pepper. Add the stock, salt and pepper and bring to the boil. Add the rosemary and bay leaf and simmer, uncovered, until the beans are tender, about an hour and a quarter. Add the potatoes and cook for a further twenty minutes. Add the courgettes and cook for a further twenty minutes. Remove the rosemary and the bay leaf and add basil and parsley.

NB for a quicker method, substitute tinned cannellini beans and/or tinned kidney beans for the dried beans and reduce initial cooking time to twenty minutes.

## Witches' Soup – Tidal Favourites

The great thing about this soup is that it is bright orange. This makes it entirely suitable for serving to witches, ghoulies and ghosts at Halloween, and, if you add plenty of garlic it will certainly keep the vampires at bay. If you call it Autumn Soup, however, it will be equally suitable for serving to right-minded people at Harvest Festival, All Saints and Guy Fawkes Night. Quantities can be varied according to how spicy-hot you like it and how large your cauldron is…

*Oil for frying*
*2 onions*
*2 large carrots*
*2 cloves of garlic*
*2 chilli peppers*
*2 orange sweet peppers*
*2 peeled, cored and chopped cooking apples*
*2 thumbs' length peeled chopped fresh gingerroot*
*The insides of 2 medium squashes or pumpkins, minus fibre and seeds*
*2 lemons, grated rind (if time) and juice*
*2 oranges, grated rind (if time) and juice*
*2 pints or so of stock, or water if you are expecting to feed vegetarians*
*Salt and pepper to taste*
*Turmeric, cayenne pepper, chilli pepper sauce and paprika, more or less, as liked*
*Crème fraîche to serve (optional)*

You can see that there's a rhythm to the ingredients: they do cast a spell, but it's a good one. Feel free to add or subtract. Adults like making faces in the hollowed pumpkins for lanterns just as much as children do.

Cover the bottom of your cauldron with oil, or oil and butter, and soften the vegetables in it, starting with the onions and chopping and adding the rest in the order given. Chobble the softened vegetables in the blender or processor until smooth, with a little stock or water to help. Return to the heat and add the liquids and seasonings. Go easy on these at first, and pep it up, as the flavour develops. Stir well and mutter incantations, blessings and messages to those with whom you wish to communicate. The soup can now rest or even freeze until you re-heat it for serving. If you are sitting down at table, a swirl of crème fraîche in each bowl is good. If you are around the bonfire ladle it straight from the bubbling cauldron into hand-warming mugs.

# Teatime

**Rosa Rugosa**

## Apricot and Muesli Bars – Linda Brewer

Makes eighteen.

*175g (6oz) butter*
*175g (6oz) soft brown sugar*
*½ teaspoon bicarbonate of soda*
*110g (4oz) Swiss Muesli*
*10g (½ oz) melted margarine*
*275g (12oz) tin apricot halves*
*Caster sugar to decorate*

Beat the butter and sugar, and then mix flour, bicarbonate of soda, muesli and salt. Brush a 20 x 30-cm (8 x 12") tin with the melted butter and spread over half the mixture. Chop the drained tin of apricots and spread on the crumb base. Cover with the rest of the crumble mixture. Bake for twenty to twenty-five minutes at 180C (350F). Cut into bars and leave to cool in tin. Sprinkle over a little caster sugar.

## Black Wet Sticky Down-in-the-Middle Gingerbread

## The Robertson Family

Came into the family through Edie's sister-in-law, and always lives up to its description.

*225g (½ lb) butter*
*225g (½ lb) soft brown sugar*
*225g (½ lb) black treacle*
*2 eggs, beaten*
*225g (½ lb) flour*
*1-2 teaspoons ground ginger*
*1 teaspoon cinnamon*
*¼ cup hot milk with 1 teaspoon bicarbonate of soda*

Cream the butter and sugar. Add the treacle and then all the other ingredients, BUT LASTLY the bicarb. Mixture. Pour immediately into a well lined 18 centimetre (7") round cake tin – the mixture is very runny – and bake at 170C (325F or gas mark 3) for one and a half hours.

## Boiled Fruit Cake – Winifred White

*225g (8oz) butter or margarine*
*225g (8oz) (1 cup) sugar*
*250ml (8fl oz) (1 cup) water*
*1 teaspoon bicarbonate of soda*
*700g (1½ lbs) mixed dried fruit*

Boil all above ingredients for three minutes. Tip into a mixing bowl. When cool, add:

*225g (8oz) (2 cups) self-raising flour*
*2 beaten eggs*
*1 teaspoon mixed spice*

Bake for two hours at 170C (325F, gas mark 3).

## Banana Cake – Wendy Turney

A good way to use up bananas that are not looking their best!

*110g (4oz) margarine*
*175g (6oz) sugar*
*2 eggs*
*2 mashed bananas*
*1 teaspoon soda*
*2 tablespoons hot milk*
*225g (8oz) self-raising flour*

Cream margarine and sugar; add beaten eggs, bananas and soda dissolved in milk. Add flour and bake at 180C (350F) for about half an hour. Fill with lemon icing, or, as we prefer it, serve as a pudding with whipped cream.

## Spiced Banana Bread – Tidal Favourites

The original version of this fragrant recipe came from my grandfather's secretary, who lived in Hawaii, where the bananas are delicious; good ripe juicy ones make the best loaf.

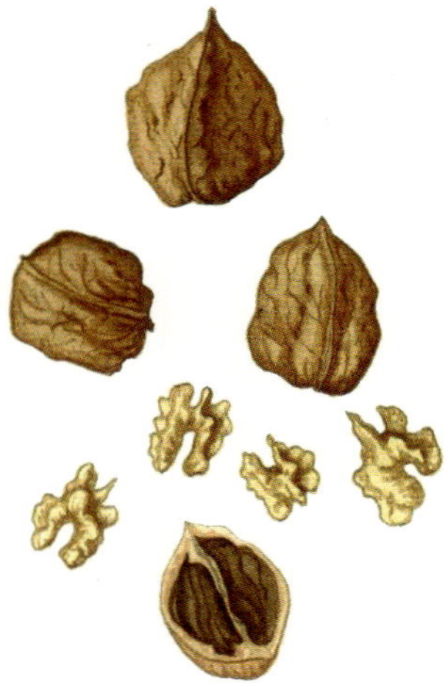

*1/3 cup (55g, 2oz) Trex*
*2/3 cup (110g, 4oz) dark brown sugar*
*2 eggs*
*2 cups (285g, 10oz) plain flour*
*3 tablespoons sour milk or plain yoghurt*
*3 large or four small mashed bananas*
*1 teaspoon salt*
*1 teaspoon baking powder*
*½ teaspoon baking soda*
*1 teaspoon ground ginger*
*½ a nutmeg, freshly grated*
*A handful of broken walnuts or pecans, if liked*

Cream the Trex and sugar; add all the other ingredients and beat well. Pour into a buttered loaf tin and bake at 180C (350F) for about forty minutes. Invert tin on a wire cooling tray and gently ease out of the tin when nearly cold. It will be almost irresistible the day it is made, but much easier to slice and butter the next day. Pieces can be warmed for a few seconds in the microwave, which will cause the butter to melt as you spread it, and the scent to be released…

## My Mother Said…

Never go anywhere empty-handed.

## Butterscotch Brownies – Tidal Favourites

It is absolutely essential not to overbake Brownies; it takes a lot of courage to remove them from the oven when they are seriously gooey. If you leave them until they spring back to the finger test, they will cool hard and dry, so check them after 10 minutes; they should be chewy on the outside and fudgey within. They probably take longer in an Aga than in a fan oven.

Melt together in a largish saucepan:

*½ cup (125g, 4½ oz) butter*
*2 cups (400g, 14oz) dark brown sugar.*

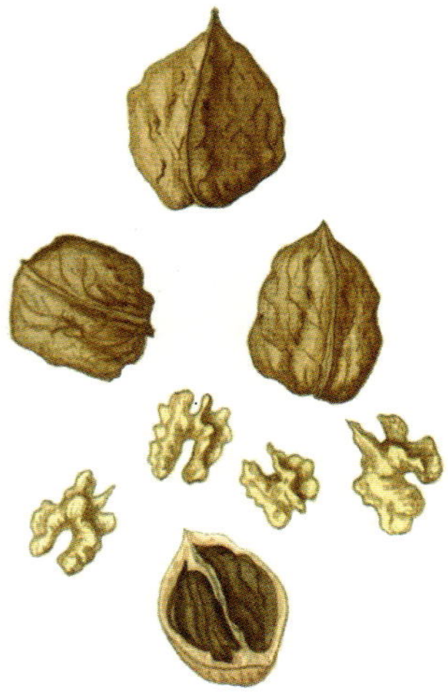

Remove from heat, and add:

*1 ½ cups (225g, 8oz) plain flour*
*½ teaspoon salt*
*2 teaspoons baking powder*
*1 teaspoon real vanilla essence*
*2 eggs*
*½ cup (a good handful) broken walnuts or pecans, if liked*

Beat all together with a wooden spoon in the old-fashioned way, most satisfying, and pour into a shallow square or oblong baking tin. Bake at 175C (350F) for 10 minutes or so; experience and knowledge of your oven will soon guide you. Cut into squares when completely cool; if this is impossible you've been a little too brave and taken them out just a bit too soon!

## Carrot Cake – Sue Bartholomew

*225g (8oz) (2 cups) plain flour*
*2 teaspoons ground cinnamon*
*1 teaspoon salt*
*3 large eggs*
*110g (4oz) (½ cup) raisins*
*450g (1 lb) (2 cups) caster sugar*
*1 teaspoon grated nutmeg*
*2 teaspoons baking soda*
*150ml (5 fl oz) (¾ cup) vegetable oil*
*700g (1½ lb) (3 cups) grated carrot*
*110g (4oz) (½ cup) chopped nuts (I use walnuts)*

Preheat oven to 180C (350F)
Grease a circular 20-cm (8-inch) tin. (I line it with greaseproof cake tin liner.)

Combine the flour, sugar, cinnamon, nutmeg, soda, salt and oil. Beat for two minutes at minimum speed. Add eggs one at a time. Beat well after each egg. Blend in carrots, nuts and raisins. Bake for one and a quarter hours, cool for five minutes and turn out.

This is delicious iced with a glacé icing made with fresh orange juice.

## Cousin Jean Jordan's Shortbread & Scrumptious Squares – Tidal Favourites

Be sure to hand plates or napkins round with this shortbread, as, though crisp, it's crumbly. It is very easy to make in the mixer.

*1 cup (250g, 9oz) slightly salted butter*
*½ cup (100g, 4oz) icing sugar, or caster sugar*
*1 ¾ cups (250g, 9oz) plain flour*
*1 teaspoon real vanilla essence (leave this out for a truly authentic shortbread)*
*½ teaspoon salt*
*Sprinkle of caster sugar*

Cream butter and sugar. Slowly add flour, then vanilla and salt. Smooth into round or square baking tray. Sprinkle with caster sugar (golden is good) and bake at 160C (325F) for about 35 minutes, until golden and crisp.

### Scrumptious Squares

Layering toffee and melted chocolate on the baked shortbread makes this an utterly over-the- top confection. Children up to the age of ninety-nine love it…

*225g (8oz) butter*
*1 large tin sweetened condensed milk*
*225g (8oz) dark brown sugar*
*4 tablespoons golden syrup*
*1 teaspoon real vanilla essence*

Put all but vanilla essence into a saucepan and stir over gentle heat until dissolved. Bring to boil and stir for five minutes. The longer you boil it, the firmer will be the toffee. Add vanilla essence and beat well. Pour over the baked shortbread and leave to cool. Melt one (or two!) bars of dark chocolate in a bowl over boiling water, and pour over the cooled toffee layer. Cut into squares, when set, with a sharp knife and a strong arm. Keeps well provided you don't let anyone see it.

## Devonshire Flapjacks – The Robertson Family

Came to us via cousins in Canada in the 30s - very easy to make (about 15-18).

*225g (½ lb) Quaker oats*
*225g (½ lb) demerara sugar*
*225g (½ lb) butter*

Melt the butter in a pan. Add the sugar and then the oats. Mix well and place in a baking tray. Smooth evenly with a fork. Bake at 190C (375F, gas mark 5) for 25 minutes or until golden brown. Allow to cool a little before cutting.

## Cut-and-Come-Again Cake – Ann Brown

This used to find great favour with my sons and their school friends. All the other mothers wanted the recipe.

*350g (¾ lb) plain flour*
*½ teaspoon salt*
*3 teaspoons baking powder*
*175g (7oz) margarine or butter*
*100g (¼ lb) raisins*
*100g (¼ lb) candied peel*
*100g (¼ lb) currants*
*200g (½ lb) sugar*
*Grated rind of 1 lemon*
*2 eggs*
*1 ½ gills (approx. 200 ml, 8 fl oz) milk*
*Strained juice 1 small lemon*

Grease a 20mm (8") tin and line with paper. Sift flour with salt and baking powder, and then rub in the fat as for pastry. Stir in the fruit and then the sugar. Beat the eggs and milk together and mix into the rest. Add the lemon juice last of all. Bake at 180c (350F) for one and a half to two hours.

## Five-Minute Sponge – Sally Pinnock

When you have unexpected guests arriving for tea in less than an hour, this will feed six to eight people and is always popular.

*4 eggs*
*6 rounded tablespoons sugar (gran or caster)*
*6 rounded tablespoons self-raising flour*
*250ml (6 fl oz) whipping cream (Elmlea if watching the waistline)*
*Strawberry jam*

Whisk the eggs and sugar together for five minutes. Meanwhile grease two sandwich tins and line with greaseproof paper if you have time… Once the five minutes are up, fold in the flour spoon by spoon. Pour the mixture into the two tins, tipping them round to cover evenly; do not spread with a knife. Place in a pre-heated oven at 190C (370F, gas mark 5), or on bottom rung of the roasting oven in an Aga. Bake for five minutes or until golden brown and the cake is beginning to come away from the edge of the tin. Turn out onto cooling racks and leave in a cool place. (The cakes can be frozen at this stage; then when they are needed in a hurry they will thaw quickly in a warm room while the cream is being whipped.) Meanwhile whip the cream until it forms soft peaks. Spread cream and jam on one sponge and sandwich the other on top. Dust with icing sugar.

## Sally Lee's Tips

**Jelly:** Make a lemon jelly with a tin of Coke or Cola – children love the fizz!

## Dorset Apple Cake – Phoebe Dooley

I was given this recipe when I came to Weymouth to live more than twenty years ago. The only part of it I have changed is the sugar: I use soft brown instead of white as I find it gives a better colour. It can be served warm with cream or cold as a cake. I like it warm.

Line an 18cm (7") round cake tin and set the oven to 150C (300F).

*175g (6oz) soft brown sugar*
*110g (4oz) soft margarine*
*2 eggs*
*110g (4oz) self raising white flour*
*110g (4oz) self raising wholemeal flour*
*1 teaspoon mixed spice or cinnamon*
*450g (1 lb) cooking apples*
*110g (4oz) sultanas*

Cream sugar and margarine. Add eggs one at a time. Fold in flour with the spice. Add the chopped apple and sultanas. (Do not add any more liquid as the apples make it moist.) Put in tin and bake for forty five to fifty minutes.

## Granny Mees' Chocolate Squares – Tidal Favourites

As with all Brownies, it is essential with this American recipe that you take them out of the oven well before you think they could possibly be done. They should be chewy to the point of gooey in the middle, and only just crisp enough to hold around the edges.

Cream together

*½ cup (125g, 4½ oz) butter*
*1 cup (200g, 7oz) caster sugar (golden or white)*

Add

*¾ cup (125g, 4½ oz) plain flour*
*2 eggs, unbeaten, one at a time*
*3 heaped tablespoons (45g, 1½ oz) cocoa*
*1 teaspoon real vanilla essence*
*½ teaspoon baking powder*
*Pinch salt*
*Handful of broken walnuts or pecans if liked*

Scrape into a square or rectangular baking tin, or into paper lined cup cake tins, and bake at 175C (350F) for ten minutes or so before inspection. Wait until cold before cutting into squares, or removing the cup cakes. A small hollow will form in the slightly under-cooked cup cakes, which is just asking to be filled with a favourite icing, such as White Chocolate Mocha; it doesn't seem to need this when cut into traditional brownie squares.

## Mars Bars Rice Krispie Cakes – Valentine Simson

Makes about twenty.

*3 large Mars Bars*
*110g (4oz) butter*
*3 tablespoons golden syrup*
*350g (12oz) Rice Krispies*

Melt the butter in a large saucepan. Add the broken Mars Bars and golden syrup and melt over low heat until it's a runny chocolate mess! Remove from heat and add Rice Krispies. Put into individual paper cases and leave to cool. Once cool put into a cake tin and hide! (They won't last long). They can also be frozen for up to one month.

## My Mother Said…

Flowers for a sick person or a celebration – send or take an arrangement or a flowering pot plant. No one has the time or the facilities to deal with cellophane, florist's ribbon and cutting stems from bed or at the beginning of a party.

## Lulworth Cove Cake – Sue Bartholomew

When we were first married we lived in a flat above a country house near Bere Regis. The cook there used to make this cake for the owner's family every week. It was a favourite of ours and became known in our family as 'Lulworth Cove cake' because of the shape it often adopted on cooling. However it is still a delicious moist everyday fruit cake.

*225g (½ lb) butter (or marg)*
*225g (½ lb) demerara sugar*
*225g (½ lb) flour*
*450g (1 lb) mixed fruit*
*3 eggs*

Cream butter, then cream with the sugar. Add eggs first (with a little flour) and then flour and fruit. If dry a little milk can be added. Bake for about one and a half hours in an oven preheated to 190C (375F) – lower gradually to about 170C (325F) – in a cake tin lined with greaseproof paper.

**Lulworth Cove**

## Myouser's Orange Cake – Tidal Favourites

My paternal grandmother was called Myouser *en famille:* she used to play pussycat games with my father that ended "now say *miaow, sir"*. Of her eight grandchildren, I was her one and only granddaughter, which I considered to be a very privileged position. Her simple but luscious Orange Cake can equally well be served at teatime (with little plates and forks) as at dinner, with pouring cream, as a pudding.

Separate:

*3 eggs (they were always free-range in her day, though she would not know the term)*

Put the yolks into the mixer bowl with:

*Grated rind and juice of 1½ large oranges*
*1 cup (125g, 4½ oz) caster sugar*

Beat until thick and creamy. Sift together:

*¾ cup (125g, 4½ oz) plain white flour*
*2 teaspoons baking powder*
*½ teaspoon salt*

Fold in to the egg mixture. Beat egg whites to a stiff froth and fold in. Pour into 2 unbuttered shallow tins, preferably with rotating sliders to ease out the cakes, and bake at 180C (350F) for about 15 minutes, or until they spring back from the finger test.

Icing:

*Grated rind and juice of remaining ½ orange – more if you like a gooey cake*
*Sieved icing sugar*

To the juice and rind add icing sugar until thick. Put between and on top of the cakes while still warm. Decorate with walnuts. The finished cake typically sinks slightly in the middle; Myouser always used to fill this hollow with extra icing to level it up. If you fail to do this, you can expect complaints from those in the know…

## Pecan and Lemon Teabread – Jennifer Halsall

I found this very good flavoured cake, which needs no butter and slices well, in a recent edition of "Home and Country", our WI magazine.

*225g (8oz) plain flour*
*1 teaspoon baking powder*
*225g (8oz) caster sugar*
*100g (4oz) butter*
*Finely grated rind of 1 lemon*
*75g (3oz) coarsely chopped pecans*
*50g (2oz) candied peel*
*2 medium eggs*
*150ml (5 fl oz) milk (ordinary or buttermilk)*
*Juice of 1 lemon*

Preheat oven to 180C (350F, gas mark 4). Grease and line a 900g (2 lb) loaf tin. Sift flour and baking powder with 175g (6 oz) of the caster sugar into a food processor. Add butter and process into fine crumbs. Tip into bowl and stir in lemon rind, nuts and peel. Lightly beat together eggs and milk and stir into dry ingredients. Spoon into prepared tin and bake for one hour, covered with greaseproof paper after forty minutes. Mix lemon juice and remaining sugar. Take cake from the oven and spoon over lemon mix. Let it cool in the tin.

(To make in the conventional way, rub butter into dry ingredients and proceed as above.)

## Porridge Biscuits – Jules Monier-Williams

*225g (8oz) lard*
*175g (6oz) granulated sugar*
*110g (4oz) butter or margarine*
*6 teaspoons hot water*
*2 teaspoons golden syrup*
*110g (4oz) porridge oats*
*225g (8oz) self-raising flour*
*Pinch salt*
*A few drops vanilla (optional)*
*Chopped nuts (optional)*

Cream fat and sugar; add dissolved sugar syrup. Work in dry ingredients and vanilla. Make into balls about one inch across (go on, guess, you youngies!) and flatten slightly onto a greased baking sheet about two inches apart. Sprinkle with chopped nuts if desired. Bake in a moderate oven until golden. When cooked, cool slightly and then lift carefully onto a wire rack until cold and firm.

## Quick Muffins for Cream Tea – Tidal Favourites

One autumn afternoon as a car full of family and friends were driving home from a blowy cliff top walk, my daughter said, "Let's stop for a cream tea at Kimmeridge like we did as children!" We were short of pennies at the time, so I promised them I would have a cream tea on the table at home, within fifteen minutes of walking through the door: a rash proposition, but we made it. One person lit the fire, another beat the cream, another laid the table, and another made pots of tea. We all stuffed our faces.

It is quickest to measure out if you have American cups and measuring spoons. Sift into a mixing bowl:

*2 cups (280g, 10oz) plain white flour*
*3 teaspoons baking powder*
*½ teaspoon salt*
*2 tablespoons (35g, 1½ oz) sugar*

Mix in another bowl:

*1 or 2 eggs, slightly beaten*
*1 cup (230ml, 8fl oz) milk*
*¼ cup (65g, or quarter of a 250g pack) butter, melted (microwave is quickest)*

Pour this over the flour mixture. Stir only enough to dampen the flour. At this stage you can vary the plain mix with nuts, dried fruit, dates, dried chopped apricots, whatever. Often plain is the most popular though. Spoon into buttered muffin tins (about two-thirds full) and bake at 200C (400F) for 12 minutes or so. This will make 18 medium buns or 12 huge ones. Halve while hot, and spread with butter, favourite jam, and clotted or whipped cream. Two of these will satisfy even greedy uncles or laid back teenagers, and toddlers will be in sticky-fingered bliss.

**Cheese Muffins** have nothing to do with cream teas, but are just the job instead of rolls or bread on picnics, with soup, or topped with various goodies for canapés. Simply add 175g (6oz) strong grated cheddar to the butter/egg/milk mix before adding it to the flour.

**Tidal Sunset**

## Rae's Lemon Cake – Sarah Pearce

My mother-in-law gave me this recipe years ago. She said it was the cake that was always left over at the end of village fetes because it looks so plain – but it is one of her most succulent and delicious, and it freezes well.

*110g (4oz) soft butter*
*175g (6oz) caster sugar*
*175g (6oz) self-raising flour, sifted*
*4 tablespoons milk*
*2 large eggs, beaten*
*Grated rind of 1 lemon*

Grease and line a 900g (2 lb) loaf tin. Pre-heat the oven to 180C (350F, gas mark 4). Cream the butter and sugar; add the beaten eggs, flour, lemon rind and milk. Mix well. Pour into the tin and smooth the top. Bake for forty to forty-five minutes, until firm.

For the syrup topping:

*3 rounded tablespoons of icing sugar*
*3 tablespoons of lemon juice*

Sift the icing sugar and mix with the lemon juice. Pour it over the cake as soon as it comes out of the oven. Leave it in the tin until it is cold. It is best left for a day before eating.

## Really Yummy Chocolate Cake – Sue Bartholomew

*225g (8oz) plain flour*
*50g (2oz) cocoa powder*
*1 level teaspoon bicarbonate of soda*
*¼ teaspoon salt*
*275g (10oz) caster sugar*
*100g (4oz) quick creaming margarine*
*150 ml (¼ pint) milk*
*2 large eggs*

Mix every thing together, then cream until smooth and soft. Bake in a lined cake tin at 180 C (350 F) for 35 to 40 minutes. Ice with this rich and slightly coffee flavoured icing:

*50g (2oz) butter*
*110g (4oz) icing sugar*
*½ teaspoon vanilla essence*
*1 teaspoon instant coffee*
*2 teaspoons cocoa*
*3 to 4 teaspoons hot water*

Mix all ingredients in food processor, gradually adding the hot water. Use double quantities (or even slightly more) to ice on top as well as in the middle.

## Rich Chocolate Ground Almond Cake – Tidal Favourites

There is no flour in this cake, which will not rise like a conventional one. The spoonful of vinegar helps to prevent the top from cracking. It is so rich that it makes a good dinner party pudding, served with cream. It is also excellent as a centrepiece for a special tea party. The best kind of baking tin to use is either a spring-form, or one with a flat sliding device that rotates round the tin under the cake.

*350g (12oz) good dark chocolate with 70% cocoa solids*
*225g (8oz) slightly salted butter*
*125g (4oz) caster sugar*
*200g (7oz) ground almonds*
*4 eggs, separated*
*1 teaspoon real vanilla essence*
*1 dessertspoon wine vinegar*
*1 small jar of apricot or raspberry jam*

Butter the baking tin, or tins, if you are using two shallow ones. Melt 175g (6oz) of the chocolate in a bowl over boiling water. Meanwhile cream 125g (4oz) of the butter with the sugar. Add the ground almonds, egg yolks, vinegar and melted chocolate, and beat well. Whisk egg whites until stiff and fold in to the mixture. Pour into tin(s) and bake at 180C (350F) for about 45 minutes. (Less, for shallow tins.) Turn upside down onto a cooling rack and ease out. The rotating arm really helps, here! As it cools put your two shallow cakes together with the jam, or coat the top of one bigger one. Melt the remaining chocolate and butter together over boiling water, stir and pour over the cake, allowing it to drizzle down the sides.

## Sour Cream Chocolate Cake – Tidal Favourites

Wickedly black and gooey and astonishingly easy to make, this cake will satisfy even the most serious chocoholics.

*2 cups (285g, 10oz) plain flour*
*1 cup (235g, 8oz) water*
*¾ cup (175g, 6oz) sour cream or plain yoghurt*
*2 cups (400g, 14oz) sugar*
*¼ cup (45g, 1½ oz) Trex*
*6 heaped tablespoons of cocoa*
*1½ teaspoons baking powder*
*½ teaspoon baking soda*
*1 teaspoon salt*
*1 teaspoon real vanilla essence*
*2 eggs*

Butter 3 layer tins. Put all the ingredients in the mixer bowl together and beat for half a minute on low speed until mixed, and then three minutes at high speed. Pour into tins and bake at 180C (350F) for about fifteen minutes. You want them just fudgey in the middle, not totally dried out. Put the layers together with any favourite jam and ice with a thick coat of butter icing:

*1 pack (250g) slightly salted butter*
*1 cup (200g, 7oz) icing sugar*
*4 heaped tablespoons of cocoa*

Cream butter and sugar; slowly beat in cocoa. You could also ice the cake with equal quantities of butter and dark chocolate, melted together in a bowl, over boiling water or covered in the microwave, well mixed and poured over while still warm.

Holly, Candle and Ribbon

## Gluten Free Fruit and Nut Cake – Trish Rudd

A real Christmas fruitcake with no flour in it at all is a great find, especially as it is both nourishing and delicious. Make it for Coeliacs and Non-Coeliacs alike; they'll all ask you for the recipe!

*250g (9oz) Brazil nuts - halved*
*225g (8oz) walnuts*
*110g (4oz) ground almonds*
*225g (8oz) seedless dates - halved*
*150g (5oz) mixed peel*
*175g (6oz) coloured glacé cherries - halved*
*75g (3oz) raisins*
*½ teaspoon baking powder*
*1 teaspoon ground cloves*
*3 medium-sized eggs*
*2 tablespoons honey*
*1 teaspoon real vanilla essence*
*3 tablespoons brandy or rum*

Put the fruit, nuts, ground almonds, spices and baking powder into a large bowl and mix together. In another bowl beat the eggs until thick and creamy; beat in the honey and vanilla. Stir into the fruit and nut mix carefully - this can get very messy. Put into a loaf tin; this amount usually fills a 900g (2lb) tin. Bake in a slow oven at 150C (300F, gas mark 2) for about 1 hour or until cake is firm to touch. Take out of the oven and pour over the rum/brandy. Keep the cake in the tin and wrap in foil over night to cool slowly.

## Grosvenor Christmas Cake – Tidal Favourites

My mother-in-law gave me this recipe soon after we got married: I had admired her Christmas cake. This was the version she always used, and so have I, changing only the type of measures; we hadn't gone Continental in Granny's day…

*225g (8oz) butter*
*225g (8oz) soft brown sugar*
*1 tablespoon black treacle or molasses*
*6 eggs*
*275g (10oz) plain flour*
*1 teaspoon salt*
*2 teaspoon mixed spice (I mix cinnamon, ground cloves, ginger and allspice; it usually comes to more than 2 teaspoons)*
*½ nutmeg, freshly ground*
*½ teaspoon bicarbonate of soda*
*350g (12oz) sultanas*
*350g (12oz) currants*
*350g (12oz) raisins*
*110g (4oz) chopped candied peel (chopped whole pieces seem to be much nicer than the tubs of ready-chopped peel)*
*110g (4oz) chopped dried apricots*
*110g (4oz) chopped glacé cherries*
*3 tablespoons milk*
*4 tablespoons sherry, rum, whisky or Cointreau. (But brandy is best of all.)*

Cream butter and sugar. Add the other ingredients in the usual way. Bake in a 23cm (9") tin, greased and lined with greaseproof paper. Insulate with more greaseproof or newspaper to prevent top and sides drying out. Put cake in cold oven, set temperature for 140C (275F). Bake for four to four and a half hours, then switch off oven and leave until cold. Next day, uncover and prick all over. Soak with more brandy, or alcohol of choice, and repeat this every week for at least 4 weeks, or until ready to ice. Traditionally, the cake should be slicked with melted apricot jam, thickly covered with ground almonds made into a paste with egg yolks and icing sugar and rolled out to fit the top of the cake, and finished with white Royal Icing, or Sugar Icing and Christmas decorations. I am never allowed to do this, as my family find icing and marzipan too sweet, so I lightly dust it with icing sugar and top with a few Christmassy bits, such as silk poinsettia flowers.

## Ground Almond Mince Pies – Tidal Favourites

If you offer these alongside the pastry versions at Christmas, you will find that they are gobbled up first every time, especially by those in the know… They are very quick to make, which is a help at Christmas time. Put in the food processor:

*150g (5oz) softened slightly salted butter*
*150g (5oz) caster sugar (golden is good)*
*2 eggs (free-range if possible)*
*150g (5oz) ground almonds*
*1 teaspoon real vanilla essence*
*Pinch salt*

Process until well mixed. Line a bun tray with paper cases (they are the devil to get out in one piece otherwise) and spoon the mixture into them. Add a spoonful of excellent mincemeat to each one, and bake at 190C (375F) for about fifteen to twenty minutes, until golden. You can also top them with an apple mix, made with *peeled, cored sliced apple tossed in a pan with melted butter, dark brown sugar and a dash of lemon juice.*

## Mince Pies

Cut circles from your Basic rolled out Pastry (page 8) with a wineglass to line patty pans. Fill with mincemeat and top with a smaller pastry circle. Brush with milk and bake. Since it's the Festive Season, rinse the wineglass, fill it appropriately and quaff. Cookie's joy!

## Mincemeat

It's incredibly easy to make, and it's much nicer than all but the most expensive bought stuff. At any time from 6 weeks to a year before Christmas, throw into a large bowl:

*All your favourite dried fruits by the (500g) packet, including chopped dried apricots, apples and pears*
*Chopped nuts are good, if liked.*

Add:

*The grated rind and juice of two lemons and oranges*
*500g or so of dark brown sugar*
*Lots of spices, such as freshly grated nutmeg, ginger, cinnamon, allspice and cloves*
*Plenty of brandy*

Traditionally, grated suet was added at this stage, but modern diets eschew it…Soak all in a plentiful quantity of brandy (not necessarily the best dinner party kind) and stir well. You will probably need most of a bottle or even more. As the fruit absorbs the liquid, add more juice or booze, until the mix is the consistency you like. Keep covered. Stir whenever you pass by its increasingly delicious aroma. This process can take days or weeks; you can go on adding brandy until your purse runs dry…If you are not using it immediately, put it into clean, dry jam jars, press clingfilm down onto the mix to exclude air and screw the jar top on. It keeps for years if you let it…

## Christmas Ice Cream

Fold some of your homemade, suet-less, mincemeat into softly whipped double cream and freeze. It makes a nice change from Christmas pud and is happily gluten free.

## Spicy Fruit and Apple Cake – Ted Lambourne

It has been difficult to choose a favourite recipe, as there are so few foods that I fail to enjoy. Perhaps I can say that this is the result of sticking in the proverbial pin! It doubles up as a quick and tasty pudding – just cut into slices, steam for one to two minutes and serve with custard. Serves ten.

*350g (12oz) dried mixed fruit*
*150ml (¼ pint) hot black tea*
*Small knob of fat or butter*
*175g (6oz) soft brown sugar*
*110g (4oz) cooking apple, diced*
*350g (12oz) self-raising flour*
*1 egg, beaten*
*2 teaspoons mixed spice*
*1 teaspoon ground cinnamon*

Soak the dried fruit in the hot tea overnight. Preheat the oven to 170C (325F, gas mark3). Line a 900g (2lb) loaf tin with greaseproof paper.

Place the soaked fruit in a bowl and add the remaining ingredients. Combine well. Transfer the mixture to the prepared loaf or cake tin and bake for two hours. When cooked, leave the cake to cool in the tin.

## Tropical Golden Fruit Cake – Angela Corran

The tropical fruit in this unusual cake makes it ideal for special occasions. It is delicious served with chunks of Cheddar or Wensleydale cheese. Preparation time: thirty minutes plus soaking time. Bake for two and a half to three hours.

*100ml (4fl oz) sherry, rum or brandy*
*110g (4oz) each of dried mango slices, pineapple, papaya and apricots, chopped*
*350g (12oz) sultanas*
*1x100g tub chopped mixed peel*
*350g (12oz) glacé cherries, roughly chopped*
*1x250g pack butter, softened*
*250g (9oz) light brown sugar*
*5 large eggs, lightly beaten*
*250g (9oz) plain flour*

Place the alcohol and fruits in a large bowl and leave to soak for up to twelve hours. Line a 23cm (9") round tin with a double layer of greaseproof paper and then tie a thick layer of newspaper round the outside of the tin. Preheat the oven to 150C (300F, gas mark2).

Cream the butter and sugar until fluffy. Beat in the eggs a little at a time. Fold in the flour and then stir in the fruit. Transfer the mixture to the prepared tin and level the surface. Bake as above, in the centre of the oven until risen and firm to the touch, and when a skewer inserted comes out clean. Leave in the tin until cold before turning out.

**Fir Cones, Candle and Ribbon**

# Tempting Toffees and Truffles

**Summer Flowers**

## Tempting Toffees and Truffles – West Lulworth WI

The West Lulworth Women's Institute wanted a speaker to demonstrate how to make toffees, fudge and truffles at one of the meetings but had no luck in finding one. It was decided that members should make and bring along their own favourites instead. Unsurprisingly, the resulting goodies were voted to be as delicious as any could be, and great fun to do. After all, who could possibly improve on WI recipes?

### Brandy Truffles – Di Stonham

Makes about 40.

*225g (8oz) plain chocolate, roughly chopped*
*150ml (¼ pint) double cream*
*50g (2oz) butter*
*350g (12oz) sponge or Madeira cake crumbs*
*2-3 tablespoons brandy*

For decoration:

*25g (1oz) vermicelli (plain chocolate)*
*25g (1oz) vermicelli (milk chocolate)*
*1 level tablespoon cocoa, sifted*
*1 tablespoon desiccated coconut*

*40 petits fours cases*

Put chocolate, cream and butter into a bowl and melt. Stir; remove from heat. Add cake crumbs and brandy. Mix well. Refrigerate the mixture until it is firm enough to handle. Shape into 40 balls, roll in vermicelli, cocoa, icing sugar or coconut, and place into paper cases.

### Chocolate Cherry Truffles – Di Stonham

Makes 32

*175g (6oz) dark chocolate*
*50g (2oz) butter*
*350g (12oz) plain cake crumbs*
*110g (4oz) icing sugar, sifted*
*2-3 tablespoons brandy or orange juice or rum*
*110g (4oz) maraschino cherries, chopped*

Make and decorate as for the brandy truffles.

## Chocolate Marzipan Log – Jen Halsall

*225g (8oz) marzipan (ready made from a whole food shop)*
*110g (4oz) dark chocolate (Bourneville)*

Cut the marzipan into three equal portions and roll each one into a log about 23 cm (9") long. Arrange the three logs together lightly (see diagram), keeping them stuck together with a little melted chocolate. Melt the chocolate over hot water and brush over the top of the log, then leave to cool. Turn over and brush underneath in the same way. Slice when firm.

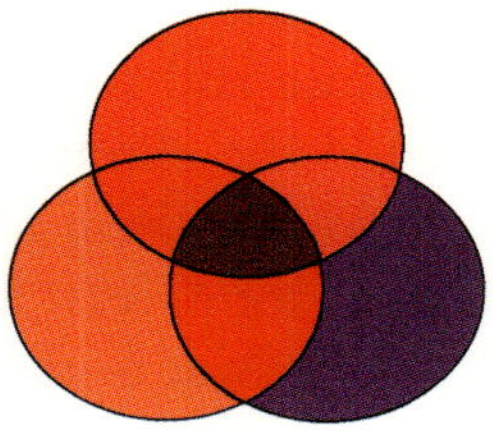

## Chocolate Cups – Di Stonham

Makes 16

*225g (8oz) dark chocolate*
*4 tablespoons strong black coffee*
*50g (2oz) butter, softened*
*½ teaspoon rum or brandy*
*1 egg yolk*
*4 tablespoons double cream, whipped*
*Flaked chocolate, to decorate*

Melt half the chocolate. Put teaspoonful in petits fours cases, to almost half full. Press another case inside each one to ease chocolate up sides of cases. Leave in fridge for at least four hours, or better still overnight. With cool hands, peel off the paper cases. Put chocolate cups in fresh cases, chill. Melt remaining chocolate with coffee. When cool beat in butter, rum/brandy and egg yolk. Chill in fridge for 2 hours. Fold in cream. Chill 30 minutes. Pipe swirls into chocolate cups. Decorate with chocolate flakes.

## Chocolate Nut Clusters – Jen Halsall

*225g (8oz) chopped mixed nuts*
*225g (8oz) dark chocolate*

Toast the nuts under a grill – watch out so they don't burn. Melt the chocolate over hot water. Stir the two together. Heap onto a tray in small spoonfuls. When set place in paper cases. This can also be made using crystallised ginger.

## Quotation

There are only three things in life that matter – good friends, good chocolate, and, oh dear, what was that other one?
*Anon*

## Soft Toffee – Ann Brown

From a chapter in a Swedish cookbook entitled "Children in the Kitchen".

*200ml (3/8 pint) sugar*
*200ml (3/8 pint) golden syrup*
*50g (2oz) butter*
*200ml (3/8 pint) double cream*
*1 tablespoon chopped almonds*

Mix sugar, syrup, butter and cream together in a heavy-based saucepan. Put on a low heat and stir with a wooden spoon for about half an hour. Be very careful not to splash the mixture about, as it will get very hot and can cause nasty burns. Put some cold water in a cup, add a few drops of the mixture and see if it sets. When you can roll it into a soft ball it is ready. Now you can add the chopped almonds, if you like them. These should have been skinned first. Stir to mix them in and then pour the toffee into little cases. Let the toffee stand and cool off for at least half an hour before tasting it. Notes: soft-ball stage is 115.5C or 240 F. It is easier to measure out the syrup if you warm the tin in the oven first.

## Celebration Dates – Dreen Meaden

*1 box of dates*
*225g (½ lb) marzipan*
*Green food colouring*
*Toasted almond flakes or 110g (¼ lb) best quality chocolate*

Pit dessert dates, cutting them lengthways halfway through. Roll coloured marzipan into a long roll and then cut off enough to fill the dates. Top with toasted almond flakes, or dip one end in melted chocolate.

## Frosted Grapes – Dreen Meaden

*225g (½ lb) each red and green grapes – ripe but firm – can be seedless if preferred*
*1 beaten egg white*
*Vanilla flavoured caster sugar*

Separate grapes into small bunches, gently wipe with damp kitchen paper. Dip in beaten egg whites and then sprinkle with caster sugar, making sure they are well covered. Place on cooling rack to dry for one or two days at room temperature.

## Frosted Rose Petals – Dreen Meaden

Separate petals ensuring that they are clean. Very gently brush with egg white and sprinkle with flavoured caster sugar, as for Frosted Grapes. Leave to dry overnight.

## Mrs Norton's Fudge – Barbara Norton's Mother-in-law, Mrs Norton Senior

*700g (1½ lbs) granulated sugar*
*110g (¼ lb) butter*
*1 tablespoon golden syrup*
*½ cup water*
*Small tin condensed milk*
*1 teaspoon vanilla essence*

Place the first four ingredients in a thick-bottomed pan and melt slowly. Add the condensed milk and bring to the boil gradually. Boil for ten minutes, stirring all the time, until the softball stage (test in cold water).
Remove from heat and add vanilla essence. Allow to cool slightly until mixture thickens and begins to grain – about seven minutes. Pour into buttered tin and cut into squares.

Other possible flavourings: mint, crystallised ginger, nuts, raisins.

## Thimbles – Elaine Knight

Makes 10

*150g (5oz) plain chocolate*
*30ml (2 tablespoons) strong black coffee*
*25g (1oz) butter*
*1 egg yolk*
*Toasted hazelnuts*
*20 sweet paper cases*

Melt half the chocolate. Place pairs of sweet paper cases inside each other. Spoon a little of the chocolate in each of the ten paired cases and spread to coat the inside thinly. Turn upside down on greaseproof paper to set.
Repeat. When firm peel off inner paper cases (the outer ones can be used to serve if they are clean enough!)
Melt rest of chocolate, beat in egg yolk and add coffee and butter. Spoon this mixture into the chocolate cases and swirl with a cocktail stick. Decorate with chopped toasted hazelnuts.

## Ronald Jack Barnett's Crystallised Gooseberries – Yvonne Adams

I found this written out in my mother's notebook by my father.

*Green gooseberries, as required*
*700g (1½ lbs) sugar*
*570ml (1 pint) water*

Use large fully-grown unripe gooseberries. Cut off the stalks and tops, cut them in half lengthways and with the point of a fruit knife remove the seeds, but leave the pulp. Boil the sugar and water together for a quarter of an hour, skim and put in a pound (450g) of the prepared gooseberries. Boil up, then simmer for a quarter of an hour. If clear and tender lift them out and allow to drain. Put another pound of gooseberries in the same syrup and when all are done spread the gooseberries out on dishes and dry them in a cool oven. When dry, pack in layers in tin boxes with waxed paper between each layer. Store in a dry place. They can be used in the same way as crystallised cherries.

# Contributors

Contributors, continued

## Recipes

# Dedication

This book is dedicated to all the lesser saints, fishers of men, who are doing great things around the Benefice, and, naturally, to Saints Andrew, Christopher, Nicholas, and to the Holy Trinity.